Venetian Academy of Indian Studies Series
No. 2

General Editor
Gian Giuseppe Filippi

Venetian Academy of Indian Studies (VAIS)

As a prestigious instrument of the Department of East Asian Studies, University "Ca' Foscari" of Venice, Italy, the Venetian Academy of Indian Studies has, since its inception, been involved with organisation of symposia, missions in field, publications, and cultural programmes that have some kind of relevance to Indological studies.

Foremost among its other academic/research concerns, however, is the VAIS' aim to promote scientific interaction and mutual understanding between Indian and European scholars, institutions, media and enterprises.

KĀMPILYA

Quest for a Mahābhārata City

KĀMPILYA

Quest for a Mahābhārata City

Edited by

Gian Giuseppe Filippi
Bruno Marcolongo

Venetian Academy of Indian Studies
Venice, Italy

D. K. Printworld (P) Limited
New Delhi, India

Cataloging in Publication Data — DK

Kāmpilya: quest for a Mahābhārata city/edited by
Gian Giuseppe Filippi, Bruno Marcolongo.
(Venetian Academy of Indian Studies series; no. 2).
Includes bibliographical references.

1. Kāmpilya (Extinct city). 2. Mahābhārata — Geography.
3. Mahābhārata — Antiquities. I. Filippi, Gian Giuseppe, 1947 –
II. Marcolongo, Bruno. III. Series: Venetian Academy of Indian
Studies series; no. 2.

ISBN 81-246-0132-1

First Published in India in 1999

Published by:

Venetian Academy of Indian Studies
Department of Indology and Far Eastern Studies
"Ca' Foscari" Venice University
Ca' Soranzo, San Polo 2169
300125 Venice (Italy)

and

D.K. Printworld (P) Ltd.
Regd. office: '*Sri Kunj*', F-52, Bali Nagar
New Delhi-110015 (India)
Phones: (011)) 545-3975, 546-6019; *Fax*: (011) 546-5926
E-mail: dkprint@4mis.com

Printed in India

Errata

Contents page:	Chap. 2:	Kampilya: One Site on More Sites? *should read as* Kampilya: One Site or More Sites?
Page 21		figure printed on this page should be shifted to page 22.
Page 22		figure printed on this page should be shifted to page 21.
Cover (Jacket) 2nd para:	6th line	Which, in trun, led . . . *should read as* Which, in turn, led . . .

Contents

Preface

Among the most eminent capitals of the Mahābhārata *Epic, is the town of Kāmpilya, which is the only one that has certainly not been identified.*

The intuition of A. Cunningham (1878), and the most recent investigations of Dr. B.B. Lal (1954-55) and Prof. V.N. Misra (1961) identified Kāmpilya in the vast mound near the small town of Kāmpil, in the District of Farrukhābād (U.P.). Nevertheless, the archaeological mission of BHU, led in 1976 by Prof. K.K. Sinha, demonstrated a very recent date of the deepest layer of the Kāmpil mound. Attracted by the solution of the problem and by my philological researches on the Mahābhārata *Epics, I accepted the invitation of the Pāñcāla Research Institute to visit the area of Kāmpil. In February 1993, I visited the impressive mound of Kāmpil along with Shree Hazari Mull Banthia, President of the Pāñcāla Research Institute and Prof. A. Mishra of the D.A.V. College of the University of Kanpur. On the basis of this first field survey, I led one of my students of the University of Venice, to prepare her thesis on the problem of the discovery of Kāmpilya. Dr. Annamaria Dallaporta, who is nowadays one of our most close collaborators, after a field mission, has confirmed the conclusions of Prof. K.K. Sinha. With the purpose of reaching a solution to the problem, we involved in our research a geo-archaeologist of international repute. With the competence of Dr. Bruno Marcolongo of the C.N.R./IRPI of Padua in remote sensing technology, our Indological investigations entered a new phase. After studying a remote sensing image of the Kāmpil area, generated by the LISS-II sensor of the Indian satellite IRS-1B, our team was able to identify a potential old human settlement. A mission organised in February 1996 by the University of Venice, the C.N.R./IRPI of Padua and the Venetian Academy of Indian Studies (VAIS), discovered a vast site of ruins, about five kilometres westward from the village of Kāmpil. The members of that expedition were Dr. Lilia Arnoldo, Indologist of the VAIS, Dr. Annamaria Dallaporta, archaeologist of the VAIS, Dr. Giovanna Fuggetta, ethnologist of the VAIS, Dr. Lucio Marcato, contract Professor of Archaeology and History of Indian Art in the University of Venice, Dr. Bruno Marcolongo, Prof. Avinash Mishra and myself. Facts of the discovery have been published in the* Bulletin of the University of Venice *("Cercando Kampilya",* Asiatica Venetiana, *1, 1996) and in the Journal of the Italian Embassy in India ("Kampilya Rediscovered",* I for Italy, *5, Sept.-Oct. 1996).*

The following mission to the same site, in February 1997, could demonstrate that the discovery consisted of a big fortified town, with the walls measuring 780 m × 660 m, orienting towards the points of the compass. On January 7, 1998, the discovery was officially presented in the Rashtrapathi Bhavan, in collaboration with the Director General of the Archaeological Survey of India, Mr. A. Shankar, and the Dean of the Faculty of Fine Arts, Banaras Hindu University, Prof. Srivastava, in the presence of the Italian Prime Minister Prof. Prodi and the Indian Minister for Human Resources Development, Mr. Bommai.

The third mission, in January 1998, confirmed the importance of the archaeological site, to which local peasants called Drupad Kilā. During this surface survey an ethnological and social investigation was conducted, which has been already published (Lilia Arnoldo e Giovanna Fuggetta, "Echi mahabharatiani in alcuni villaggi dell'Uttar Pradesh", Quaderni Asiatici, *4.4.1998). Also a first evaluation of the antiquity of the site was done too. Actually, the bricks and the terracotta fragments scattered on the surface could be traced to a date variable between the sixth century* BC *and the first century* AD*. The excavations in collaboration with our Indian colleagues will be in a better position to determine this point, and to check the underlying potentialities therein. While talking about this project with the Director of the Excavations of the Archaeological Survey of India, Dr. Bisht, on January 28, 1998 we were surprised to find that the dimensions and the orientation of the Drupad Kilā coincided exactly with those of Dholavira, a mature Harappan town, excavated by the eminent archaeologist. One can see in the present publication, that the maps of these two ancient cities overlaps* *(see page no. 13)**. This evidence could demonstrate a continuity of urban models from the Harappans until the Kuṣāṇa's times, following a shift of human settlements from the missed course of Sarasvatī towards Doāb. If Drupad Kilā is the superficial trace of Kāmpilya, as several clues suggest,* *we are able to obtain another element against the old "Aryan Invasion Theory".*

It is well known that Doāb, the region included between rivers the Ganges and the Yamunā, has been the cradle of the Indian Civilisation since Vedic times. During Epic times the South Pāñcāla covered the centre of Doāb, with the fabulous capital of King Drupad at Kāmpilya. In the present day, this area corresponds to Districts of Eṭāh, Mainpurī, Farrukhābād, Eṭāwāh and Kānpur in the State of Uttar Pradesh. We indicate the geographical territory of Kāimgañj, comprehending it to be the area of Kāmpil-Rudāin, the place where Kāmpilya flourished. From the most remote antiquity, this region has been celebrated for its peculiar historical features. The communities were multi-ethnic and well integrated, organised in confederations of villages and tribes, with an administration based on assembly system. The pacific and prosperous situation of the South Pāñcāla favoured the appearance of charismatic leaders and seers, mentioned in the Hindu, Jain and Buddhist literatures. These features have been preserved from the middle ages to the present day, though some decadence has been produced by the shifting of the geopolitical centre of India, done mostly under the Mughal and the British dominations. But even in the present day, the integration of the multi-ethnic communities is evident in that area, with integration of tribes in the villages and a good acceptance of democratic rules. At the same time the area has produced political leaders and intellectuals too.

On the basis of evidences from researches done in fields of humanities and sciences through new technology, we have realised that the Kāmpilya area can be a model for the human sciences for peaceful coexistence, preservation of tradition, but with an open attitude to external cultural data, denoting a great human potentiality. In this way we amplify the conception of geo-politics prevalent in that geo-civilisation, with a new possible historical interpretation.

In this perspective, beyond the archaeological event, the team led by Dr. Marcolongo and myself has created a big "Kampilya Project" with three precisely defined targets:

- *to promote an analytical multi-disciplinary investigation on the Kāmpilya area (in the Kāimgañj* tahsīl, *District of*

Farrukhābād, U.P.) utilising new technologies. The Indian and the European researchers, in this way, will cooperate in the circulation of instruments, methodologies and technical know-how as well as in opening up of both academic and commercial communications. The objectives of the investigation consist in a planning for the recovery, preservation, optimisation and development of the agricultural, environmental, cultural and communicative resources. The elaboration of this project goes through a network of Universities and Research Institutions, Local Authorities, Small-Medium Enterprises and Media;

- *to create a web of economic interests between European and Local Enterprises, for positive exploitation of the rich potentialities of the area, in the framework of respect for environmental and cultural ecology. Apart from the reciprocal commercial satisfactions, the purpose of this web entails practical achievement of social and economic promotion of the Kāmpil area, as planned in the previous point; and*
- *to carry out a proper circulation of information through the popular media, multimedia, scientific journals, for better mutual comprehension, in order that the European and Indian operators might work together with a growing spirit of confidence. The dissemination of the multi-disciplinary results of the "Kampilya Project" will constitute an important instrument increasing the contacts between India and Europe.*

My experience of field research for nearly thirty years in India suggests that the best channel for human contacts is culture. Culture is a universal value, able to instil noble feelings and thoughts in human soul. "Kampilya Project" wishes to become the container for this cultural exchange. With regard to myself, this initiative will be an opportunity for returning to Mother India some spiritual gifts that She offered me with generosity for a long period.

Gian Giuseppe Filippi

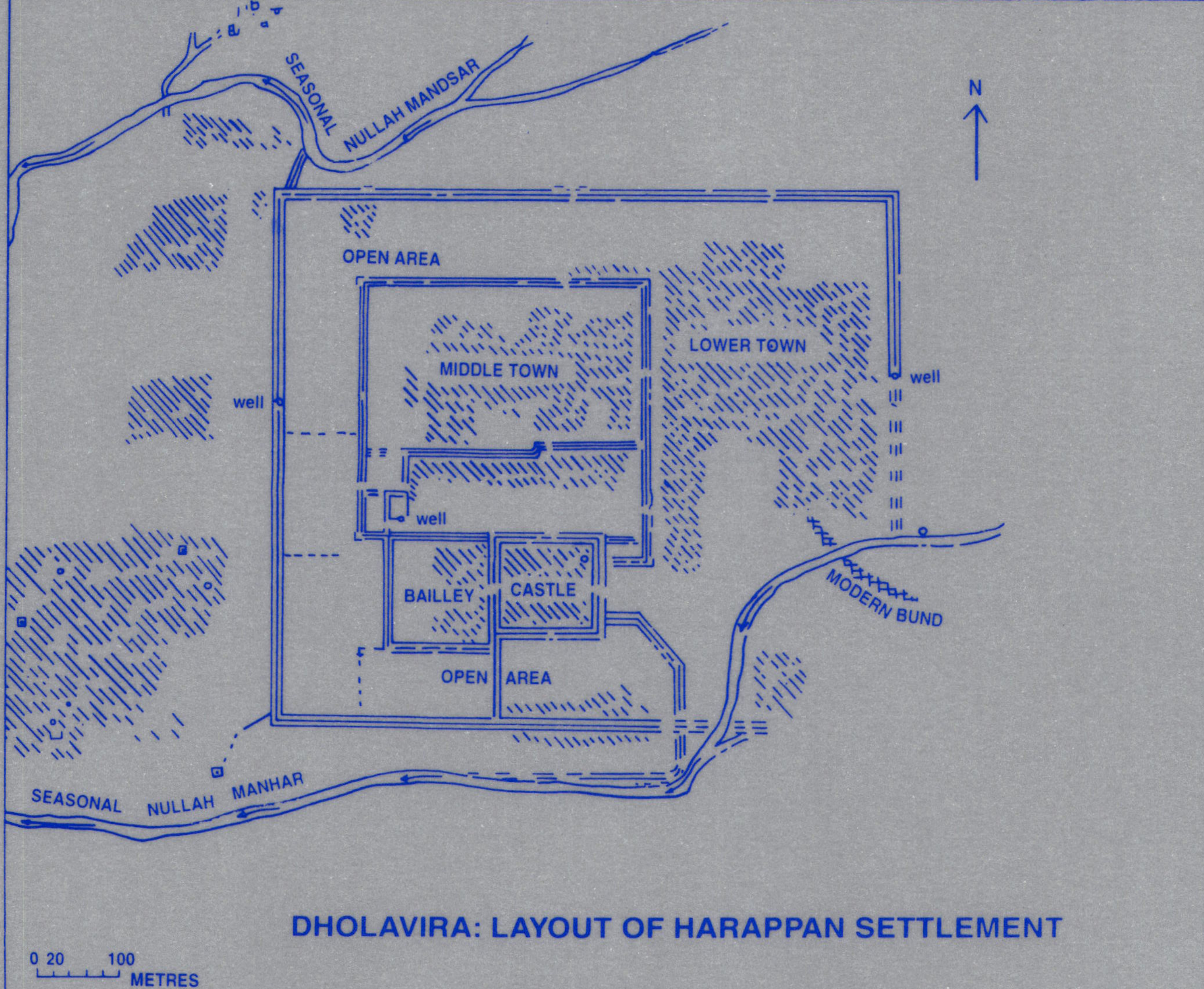

DHOLAVIRA: LAYOUT OF HARAPPAN SETTLEMENT

(Ref. Lal. B. B. : The Earliest Civilization of South Asia. 1997. p.138)

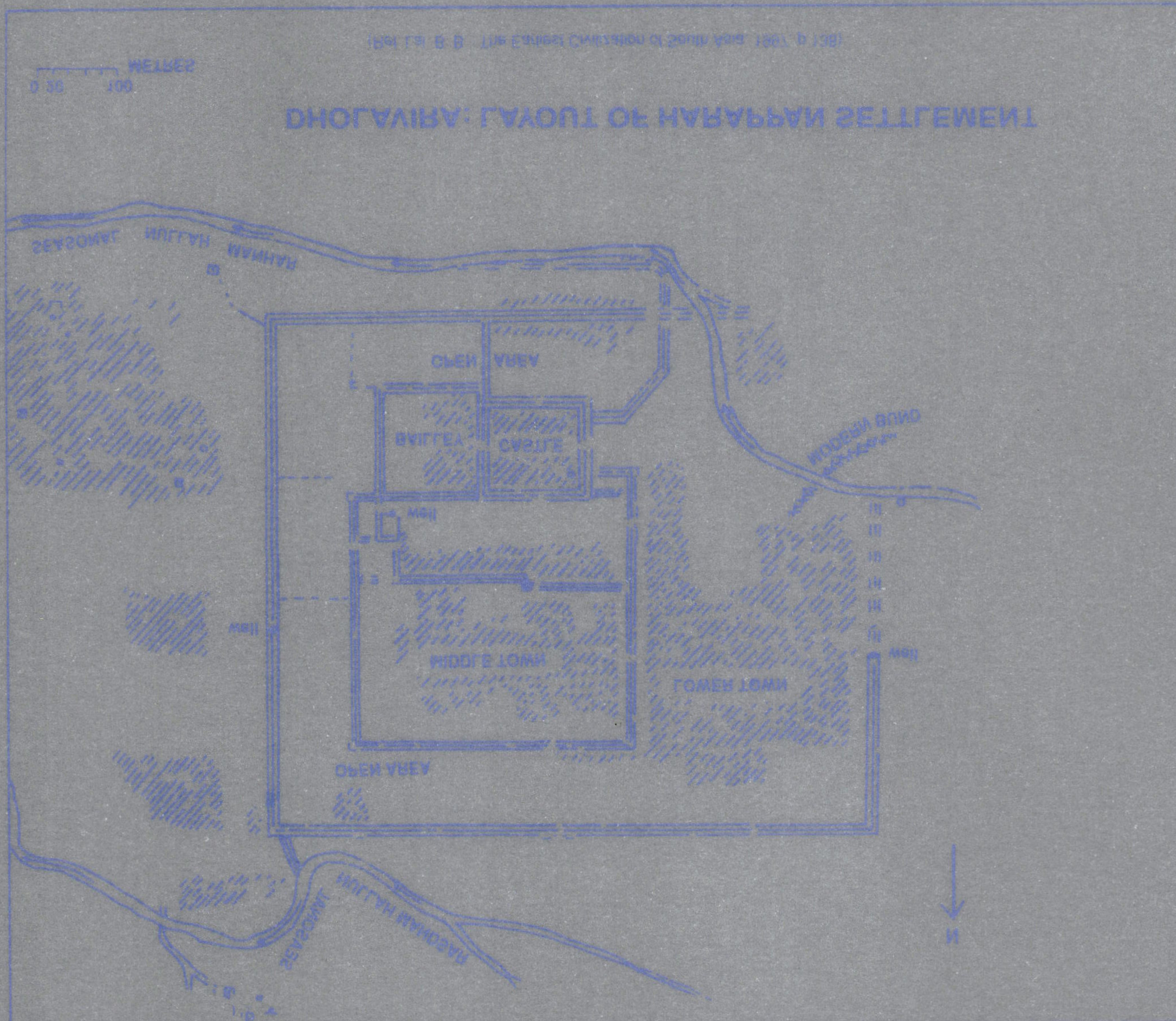
DHOLAVIRA: LAYOUT OF HARAPPAN SETTLEMENT
(Ref. Lal, B. B. : The Earliest Civilization of South Asia, 1997, p. 138)
0 35 100
METRES
SEASONAL NULLAH MANHAR
SEASONAL NULLAH MANSAR
MODERN BUND
OPEN AREA
BAILEY
CASTLE
Well
MIDDLE TOWN
LOWER TOWN
OPEN AREA
N

Map of "DRUPAD KILA"

(from topographic survey)
Feb. 1997
B. MARCOLONGO

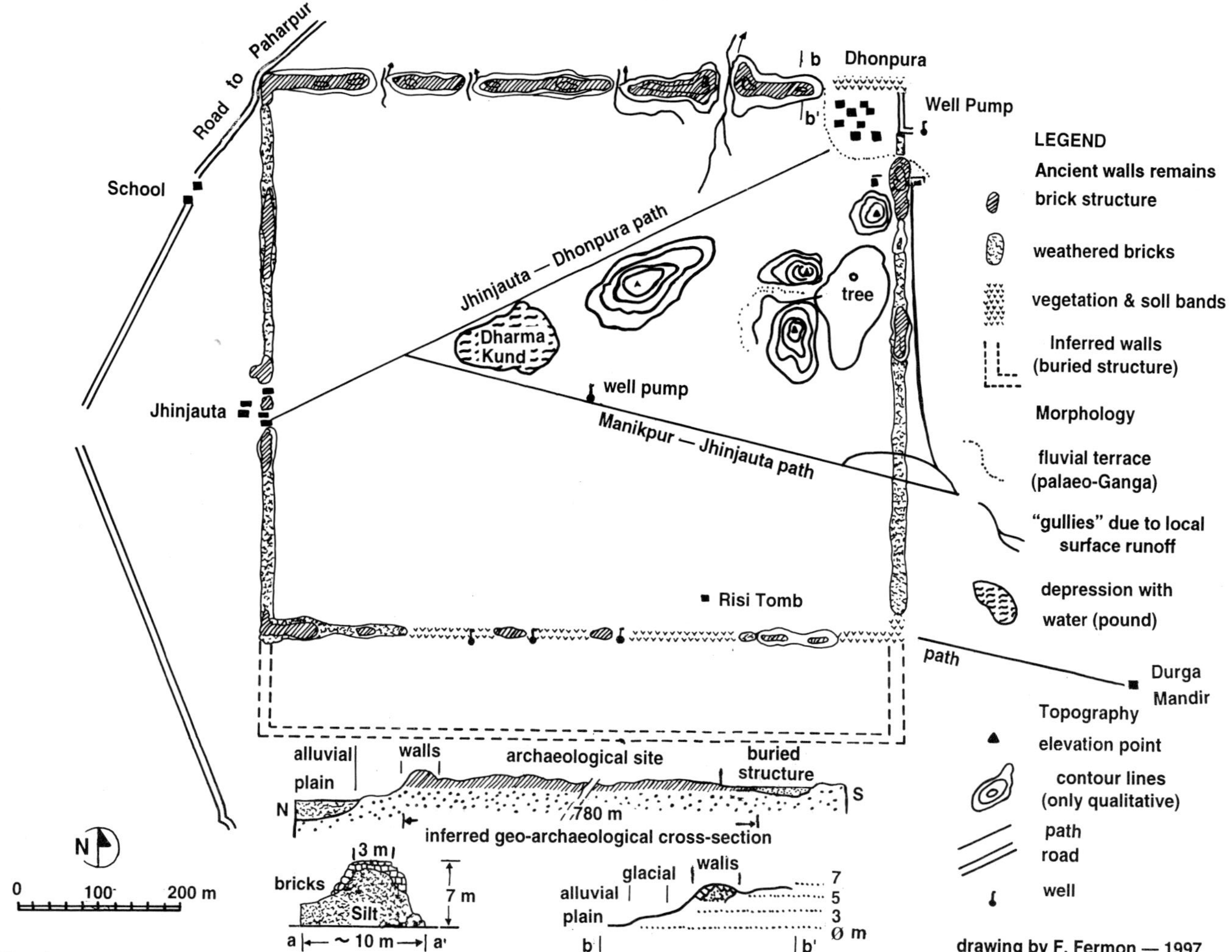

drawing by F. Fermon — 1997

1

Geoarchaeological Observations in Doāb Plain

Through Advanced Remote Sensing Methodology

Bruno Marcolongo

LANDFORMS and their evolution in space and time, as well as availability of natural resources in terms of water, soil and raw materials, have influenced strongly ever, organisation and development of human settlement models. That is quite clear, since the middle Holocene (about 6,000 years BC, after a pluvial phase and before the beginning of a period of progressive climatic drying up) in the broad fluvial plains became the cradle of most ancient urban civilisations, such as that of Nile, Tigris-Euphrates and Indus-Ganges.

The vast territory of fluvial plain lying in the Indian sub-continent at the foot of the Himālaya range has been and even today is affected by neotectonics, with differential tilting of the land surface and hence consequent significant changes of channel characteristics and river's direction of flow during late Pleistocene-Holocene. Moreover, even climatic variations with glacial and inter-glacial phases and thereby derived sea level fluctuations contributed to this instability of general hydrographic network.

In the last few decades, numerous Indian and foreign scholars in various disciplines have worked on this active foreland basin, constituted by the Indo-Gangetic plain, where sedimentation is taking place by fluvial processes. Among other things, it has been stressed that there is neotectonics control on the middle stretch of Ganges near Kanpur (U.P.), where the river is shifting towards SE attracted by a normal fault, the so-called "Moradabad fault", with strikingly NW-SE parallel to orogen (V.N. Bajpai, 1989 ; Indra Bir Singh & V.N. Bajpai, 1989; Indra Bir Singh,

V.N. Bajpai, A. Kumar & M. Singh, 1990 ; B. Parkash & S. Kumar, 1991). Furthermore, imposing changes have been recognised in river courses in Haryana, Punjab and Rajasthan due both to neotectonics and climate with abandonment of global western flow direction (Ghaggar-Sarasvatī receiving contributes of palaeo-Yamunā-Dṛśadvatī) and creation of a new generalised southward flow direction which is mainly represented by the present Yamunā (Y. Pal, B. Shahai, R.K. Sood, & D.P. Agrawal, 1984; H.P. Francfort, 1984; P. Gentelle, 1984; V.N. Misra, 1993; G. Fuggetta & B. Marcolongo, 1994; S.P. Gupta, 1994-5; D.P. Agrawal *et al.*, 1994-5; B. Marcolongo & M. Tosi, 1995).

On the other hand, this area has been the seat for rising and development of the Harappan culture and so, necessarily, the ancient sites' distribution over the whole region must be inserted from a diachronic perspective in a palaeoenvironment quite different from the present one. Also the migrations, which during the second millennium BC brought a considerable number of people to settle down in the Ganges' alluvial plain, could have a probable pre-existing cause in the grand hydrographic upsetting coinciding with the diversion of Yamunā's course from west to south. This river, therefore, seems to play, in this evolutive context, the role of tongue for the partition of noticeable discharges between Indus and Ganges watershed.

Fig. 1 gives a synthetic overview of principal evidences of Quaternary palaeohydrography and its trends in the Indo-Gangetic basin, mostly elaborated in the cited bibliography.

The present geoarchaeological research, carried on since 1995 in the central Doāb plain around Kāmpil village (long. 70° 16'40" East and lat. 27° 36'40" North, Farrukhābād district, U.P.), is totally inserted in this palaeohydrographic framework. Its demand arose from the necessity of completing of both the archaeological sites' pattern, mainly looking for the possible identification of Kāmpilya town, and the hydrographic evolutionary picture during pre- proto and historical times of Yamunā-Ganges system in this central stretch of their course. Thus, this integrated approach is intended to guide, on the one hand, the field survey, by means of propedeutic thematic maps preliminarily deduced from remote sensing and ancillary data, and on the other hand, to describe and interpret archaeological evidences in their natural setting.

At the beginning a thesis study developed jointly at the Department of Indological and Far East Studies/University "CàFoscari" of Venice and Institute of Applied Geology/National Research Council of Padua, on Kāmpil mound and its surrounding territory, which brought to light among other things the existence, south-west of the present Ganges right bank, of a series of palaeoriver-beds, recognisable in the field in the shape of elongated natural sandy levees, south-west of the right bank of the present Ganges. These characteristic landforms with their gently meandering spatial distribution and relative angular discontinuities indicate a process of local migration of the Ganges towards the present flood plain (north-east), the outermost course being the oldest one (*fig.* 2).

On taking an attempt for achieving morphogenetic correlation with the geomorphic features described by Indra Bir Singh, V.N. Bajpai, A. Kumar and M. Singh (see bibliography), the palaeoflow directions here numbered 0, 1, 2 and 3 appeared to be situated on the so-called T_2 surface.[1]

On the contrary, palaeoflow direction 4 is lying on T_1 surface.[2] The limit between the two genetic surfaces is marked by an almost continuous fluvial terrace, with an escarpment of 5-10 m of height running parallel to the present-day Ganges' course (*fig.* 3).

These palaeohydrographic elements create noticeable morphological discontinuities, breaking the monotony of a relatively flat landscape and they must have exerted ever since there is a strong attraction for the human settlement in terms of topographic prominence and availability of natural resources (shallow ground-water resources and more fertile soil in correspondence to the sandy-silty natural levees). As a matter of fact, many sites in this area, with acknowledged archaeological evidences, at least dating back to the iron age, appear distributed along the just mentioned fluvial terrace (e.g., Auraṅgābād, Bhargain, Bilsārī, Kāmpil, Rāipur Mothra, Biṭhūr, Bhojpur, Jājmau). Therefore, conceptually speaking, a possible existence of older sites could be inferred further to the west.

Certainly, the verification of this kind of tight interdependence of man and environment has stimulated the elaboration of a theoretical model of distribution and localisation of ancient settlements, in connection with peculiar palaeoforms. The model guided a geomorphological survey that was done in the area of interest in February 1996. It was prepared by a propedeutic interpretation of Indian satellite multispectral images from IRS-1B[3] which allowed to build a thematic map, showing places that could bear archaeological remains. Very soon this approach led to the discovery of a wide archaeological complex, organised around a walled town locally named Drupad Kilā (long. 79°12'30" East and lat. 27°36'10" North, 7 km to the W-SW from Kāmpil).

During a successive field campaign in February 1997, a detailed geomorphological map has been realised, with the main aim of describing relations between the archaeological complex and palaeo-Ganges' course.

The satellite data have been recently interpreted and a more accurate analysis of an enlarged portion of the IRS-1B scene at scale 1:25.000 allowed to recognise other significant mounds in the neighbourhood of Drupad Kilā, especially one near the village of Nārāyaṇpur called by the peasants, 'Ghadi Fortress' (about 1 km north-west from the centre of Drupad Kilā). (*fig.* 4).

The most outstanding geomorphic features deduced from IRS-1B images, checked with topographic elements from official cartography (1 : 25.000 and 1 : 50.000 maps) and ground observations, are in the studied area (*fig.* 5) :

- a principal fluvial terrace, bordering the T_1 surface of the Ganges valley, on top of which is situated the "Drupad Kilā" complex ;
- a secondary and likely younger terrace flanking the southern portion of the walled town;
- a major palaeo-Ganges' flow direction with meandering behaviour, which presents a bifurcation just in front of the village of Māṇikpur (500m east of Drupad Kilā);
- a minor episode of palaeo-flow intercepting the southern band of Drupad Kilā.

The major palaeocourse can be correlated to the earlier mentioned natural levee no. 4. Thus, in a chronological context it appears one of the most recent among the various palaeo-fluvial traces and it must have been active during middle-recent Holocene, probably till protohistoric and historic times. A further passage in the progressive shifting of Ganges towards north-east is witnessed by the historical course of Būḍhīgaṅgā Nadī, few km far from it in the alluvial plain.

Its morphogenetic action is responsible for the incision of the escarpment standing from a few meters of height up to 10 m above the present-day flood plain. This escarpment cuts the north-east corner of Drupad Kilā, thus clearly indicating that the Ganges was still flowing there during the life of the site[4] and probably caused its abandonment, at least as a stable and organised settlement, after a series of ruinous floodings.

The minor palaeo-flow direction, meandering from west to east in the southern portion of the area, is an evidence in favour of one or more over-bank floods which could have destroyed and buried, under few meters of fine sediments (silty and clayey sand), a band of Drupad Kilā, whose width could be inferred to be about 120 m. In other words, an older site could have been extended over a square of 780 m of side, while a younger one could have been reduced to a rectangular shape of 780 × 660 m^2.

In synthesis, the morphogenetic activity of the local major palaeo-Ganges was characterised earlier by flooding and deposition, then by erosion and sediment transportation and at the end by marked shifting of the riverbed.

Most of the mounds identified around Drupad Kilā are also lying along the edges of the fluvial terrace and that is particularly true for the so-called Ghadi Fortress, whose position seems to control a nearly shallow water ford across the old Ganges' course.

Contextually with this geomorphological and geo-archaeological survey, a very detailed topographic survey of Drupad Kilā has also been performed (*fig.* 6).

A special attention was paid to the description of the shape and state of preservation of the town-walls. Actually the legend of *fig.* 6 proposes various categories concerning outcrops of baked bricks and weathered baked brick structures, narrow bands of discontinuities in vegetation cover and soil and bands of buried baked brick structures.

The north-facing wall is best preserved, still standing up 6-7 m over the adjacent alluvial plain. Its variable thickness from

3 m on the top to about 10 m at the bottom, is due to weathering processes (erosion and deposition), which have also caused cutting of gullies through the whole thickness of the structure. Nevertheless, a major ravine developed by surface runoff, 200 m to the west of Doṇpurā village, seems to have been guided by a wall discontinuity like a monumental door locally witnessed by the presence of two larger buttresses in the body structure itself. Along the western side, preserved stretches of the brick structure are encountered at 250 m north from Jhinjauta and at just the eastern entrance of the same village, where traces of buttresses have been surveyed too. More discontinuous tracts of brick structure signs are seen on the southern and eastern sides.

Many mounds of variable sizes and heights are scattered inside Drupad Kilā. For the moment, only a few among the most developed ones have been reported on the map; nevertheless, all are located in the north-east quarter, maybe indicating there both a concentration of major public buildings and a longer and more important residential occupation. In this part, due to relatively higher relief energy generated by thicker anthropic layers, the pluvial and surface runoff erosion has cut deeply into the terrain forming a local terrace and small talweg.

The north-east corner of the baked brick walls, as previously alluded, appears destroyed to a length of about 100 m along north side and 80 m along east side. A terrace escarpment delimitates the anthropic deposits, as an expression of late morphogenetic remodelling of major fluvial terraces before the definitive abandonment of the Ganges' older flow direction.

A pond of elliptical shape, covering about 1 hectare with shallow water, is a prominent feature about hundred meters to west-north-west from the centre of the walled town. It can be suggested that, although precise altimetrical and hydrological measures are for the moment missing, this water body is formed with the local groundwater emergence. It may be a perched phreatic aquifer lodged in the alluvial deposits underlying Drupad Kilā structures. That is, this peculiar reservoir must have characterised the site ever since, taking into account only probable variations in extension due to groundwater surface fluctuations.

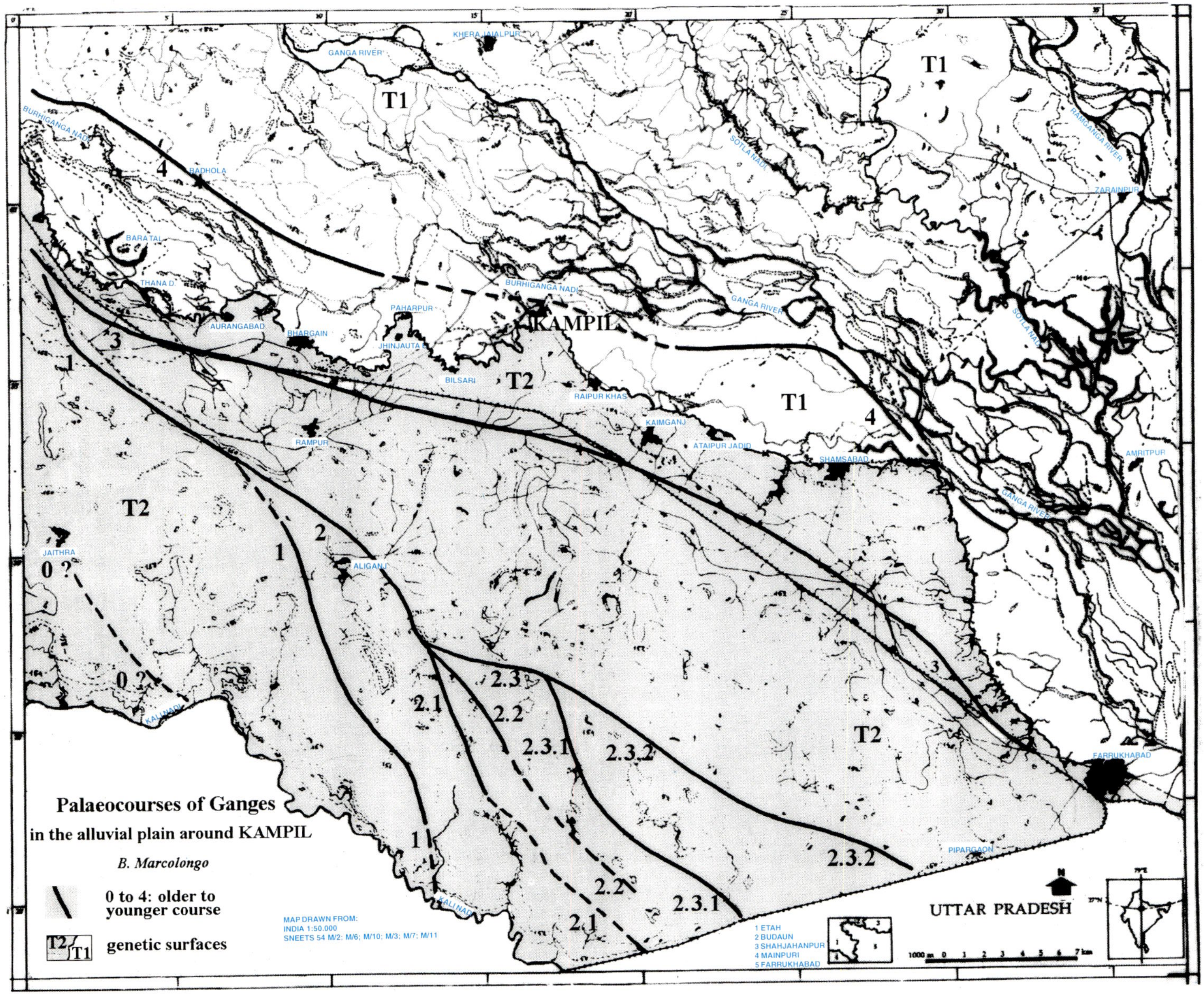

fig. 1 : Quarternary Palaeohydrography between Indus and Yumuna.

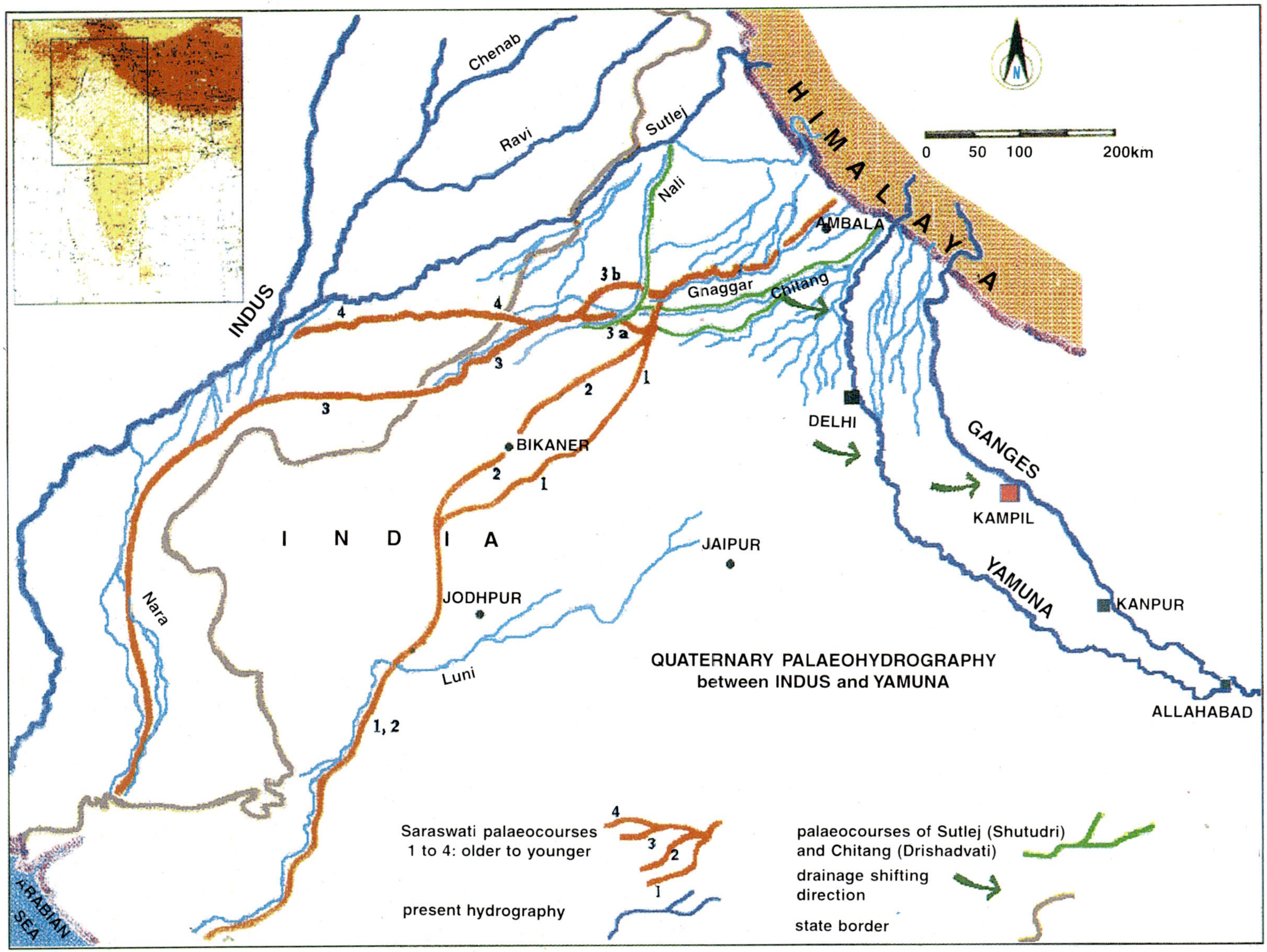

fig. 2 : Palaeocourses of Ganges in the alluvial plain around Kampil.

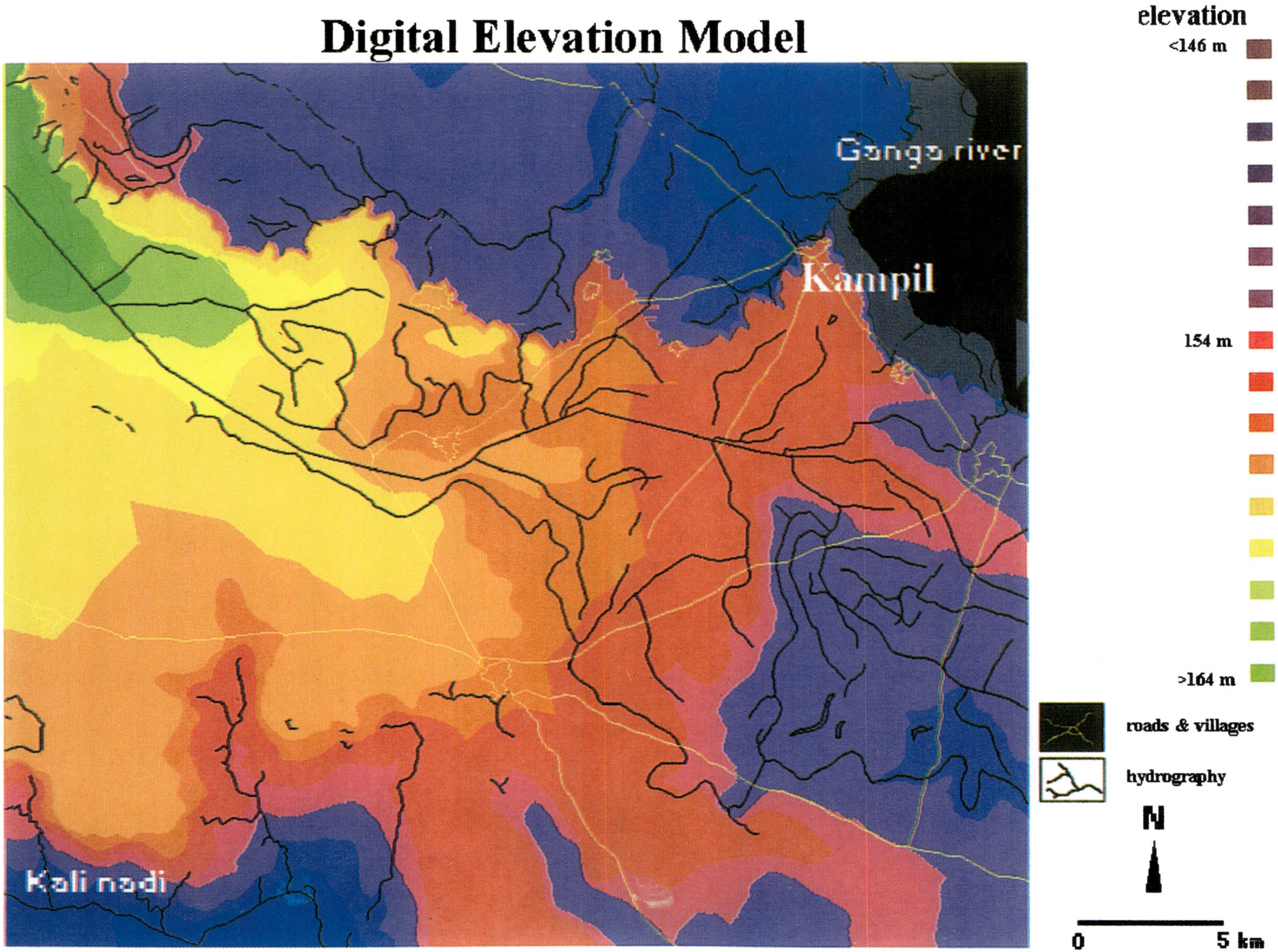

fig. 3: Digital Elevation Model.

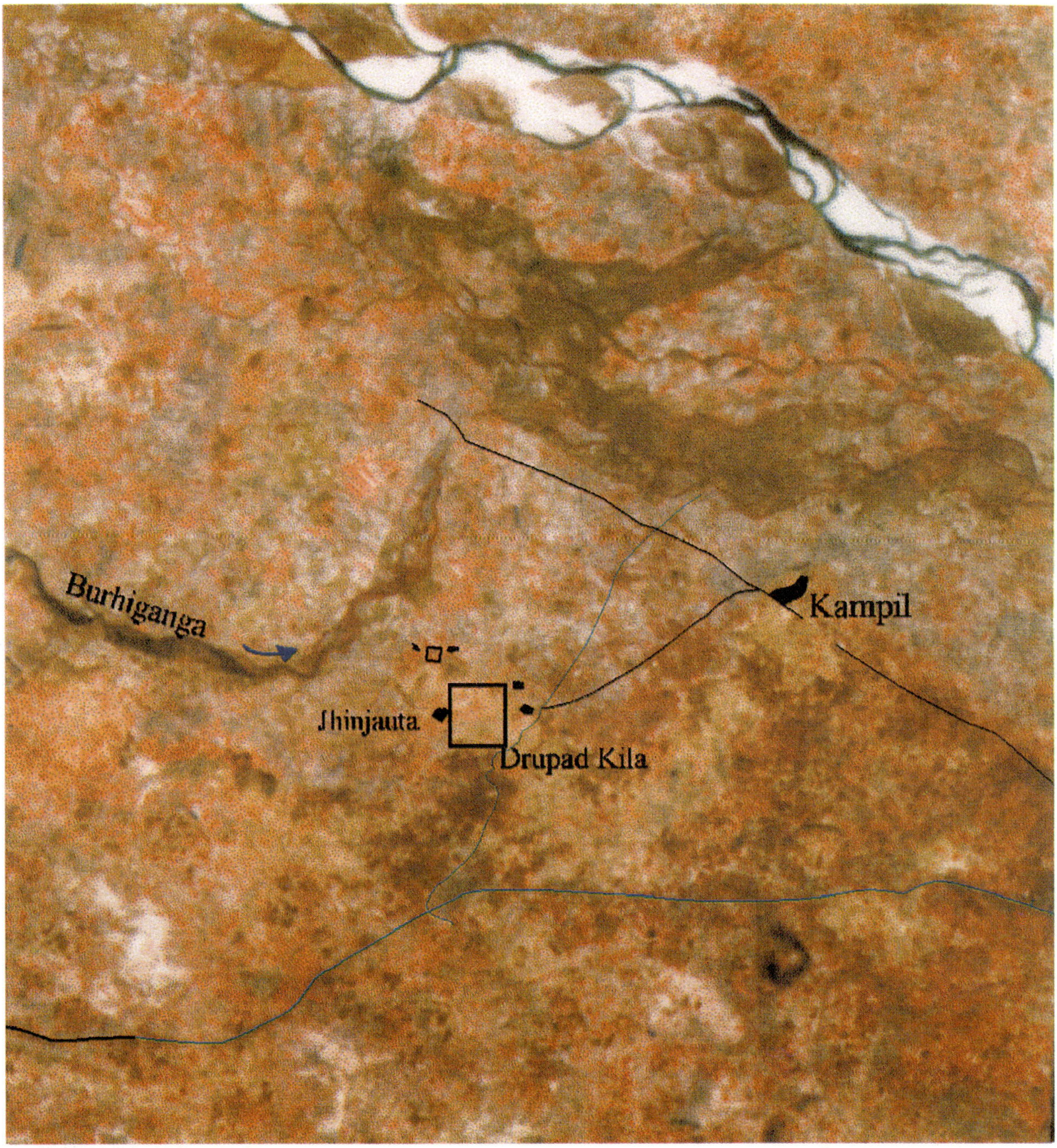

fig. 4: Portion of IRS 1B scene (false colour composition) covering the alluvial plain around Kampil.

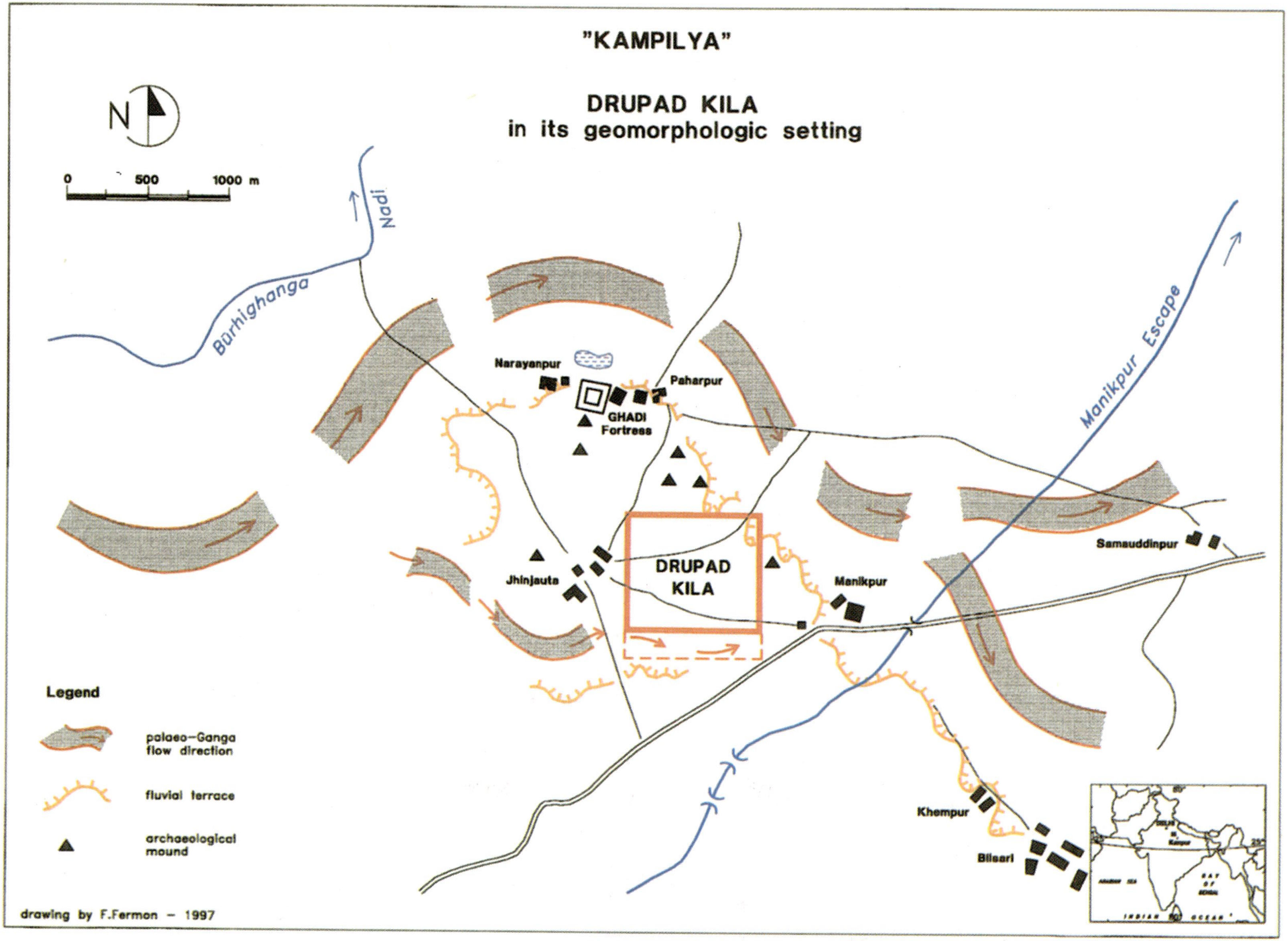

fig. 5: Drupad Kilā in its geomorphologic setting.

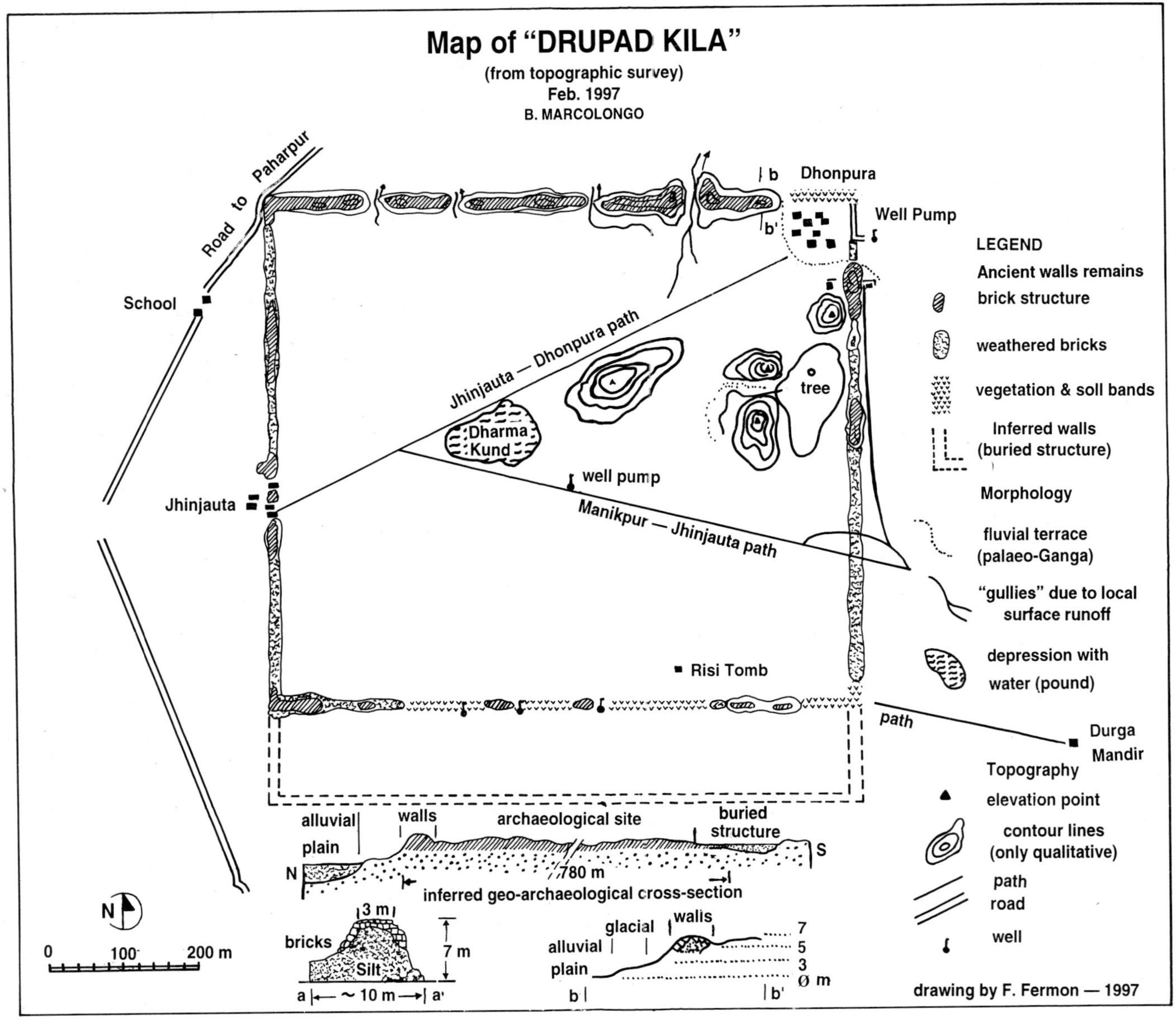

fig. 6: Map of "Drupad Kilā" (from topographic survey).

A geo-archaeological cross-section from north to south attempts to reconstruct the relations between natural and anthropic layers. Alluvial plain, mainly filled by sand and silty sand, is cut in the older T_2 silty clay deposits, over which the Drupad Kilā was built. In the southern portion a thin cover of younger silty sand alluvium probably conceals deeper archaeological evidences belonging to an earlier Drupad Kilā settlement and also spreads over T_2 sediments. Other two small profiles sketch the walls' structure and the relative height over the site surface of the alluvial plain.

All these interpretative elements form a coherent set of data for further development of the study, which has to consider both a stratigraphic deepening in the site spot and a regional analysis of the natural characteristics and archaeological evidences of the whole Doāb plain. Local stratigraphic analysis, to be performed by geognostic, geoelectric and geo-radar soundings on trenches, will allow to check, among other things, the possible presence of fluvial episodes intercalated to levels of human occupation. So, the fluvial history of Drupad Kilā area will be correlated to the history of the ancient site itself and also inserted in the general palaeohydrographic evolution of the broad Yamunā-Ganges alluvial plain.

Here the proposed geo-archaeological approach will integrate data from bibliography, new IRS-1C/D satellite images at higher resolution and detailed geomorphological and hydrogeological field survey. At the end, the results obtained from two main thematic fields, that is environment and cultural resources, will be intersected for recognising the reciprocal influences of man and environment at that time. Thus it will provide Public Authorities with useful tools of knowledge for future management and plan of actions.

Bibliography

Bajpai V.N. (1989), Surface and sub-surface evidences of neo-tectonics and the aquifer disposition in central gangetic alluvial terrain of Kanpur-Unnao region in Uttar Pradesh, India. "Photonirvachak", *Journal of the Indian Society of Remote Sensing*, Vol. 17, No. 2, New Delhi.

Bajpai V.N., Gokhale K.V.G.K. (1986), Hydrogeomorphic classification of the Marginal Gangetic Alluvial plain in Uttar Pradesh, India, using satellite imageries. *Journal of the Geological Society of*

India, Vol. 28, No. 1, Bangalore.

Bajpai V.N., Prabhakar C.P. (1993), *Over exploitation of aquifers in the vicinity of the river Yamunā : a case study on a part of Delhi region*. Proceedings of the "National Seminar on Hydrological Hazards, Prevention and Mitigation", Roorkee.

Dallaporta A., Filippi G.G., Marcolongo B. (1996), *Cercando Kāmpilya*. "Asiatica Venetiana", 1, Dip. Studi Indologici ed Estremo-orientali, Università "Cà Foscari", Venezia.

Dallaporta A., Filippi G.G., Marcolongo B. (1996), *Kāmpilya Rediscovered*. "I for Italy", Year III, n. 5, Italian Embassy, New Delhi.

Indra Bir Singh, Bajpai V.N. (1989), Significance of Syndepositional Tectonics in Facies Development, Gangetic Alluvium near Kanpur, Uttar Pradesh. *Journal of the Geological Society of India*, Vol. 34, Bangalore.

Indra Bir Singh, Bajpai V.N., Kumar A., Singh M. (1990), Changes in the Channel Characteristics of Ganga River during Late Pleistocene-Holocene. *Journal of the Geological Society of India*, Vol. 36, Bangalorc.

Marcolongo B., Tosi M. (1995), *Il fiume scomparso. La Sarasvati nell'età del Bronzo : da disastro ecologico a fonte di salvazione*. "Saecularia Nona", Annual 12, Università degli Studi di Bologna, Bologna.

Parkash B., Sudhir Kumar (1991), The Indogangetic Basin. In Tandon S.K. *et al.*, *Sedimentary basins of India : tectonic context*, Gyanodaya Prakashan Publ., Nainital.

References

1. The Indian authors define it as ". . . the regional plateau or upland surface making extensive interfluves, present on either side of the Ganga River valley. It is 10-20 m above the present-day flood plain and major part of this surface shows silty clay, often with *kaṅkar* development. There are many abandoned drainages and abandoned meandering channel belts, some of which have been converted to lakes and ponds. The active channels of this surface are of entrenched meandering type and carry essentially silty fine sand. Channel characteristics of these abandoned channels are in strong contrast to the present-day active channels over this surface. The abandoned channels show large and tight meander loops. Within tens of meters below this surface, no major sand bodies are present in the sub-surface. Age of this surface may be the last major interglacial (~120 ka), upon which tens of meters of sediments have accreted ever since; the age of abandoned

drainages is 5-10 ka" (Singh, 1987; Ghosh & Singh, 1988).

2. The Indian authors define it as ". . . surface located about 5-10 m above the present-day Ganga River flood plain T_0 and restricted within the river valley. Small yazoo-type drainages often parallel to the main Ganga channel are developed. It shows extensive vegetation and number of ponds and lakes. Near-surface sediments are silty sand; but below a few meters, thick sand deposits are present. In the aerial photographs and imagery, this surface shows many meander scars and scroll bars. They are well developed near Kanpur and between Mirzapur and Ghazipur. It implies that when the Ganga River was flowing at T_1 surface it was highly sinuous. The age of T_1 surface abandoned meandering channel is conceptually inferred to be around 20-30 ka, the last interglacial" (Ghosh & Singh, 1988).

3. Two scenes have been obtained from National Remote Sensing Agency (NRSA) in Hyderabad. Acquired by IRS satellite on December 1993, they are respectively identified by Path 28/Row 48 and Path 27/Row 48. These data have been elaborated with 'Idrisi' software for thematic interpretation (geomorphology, land use, archaeological evidences) utilising various modules as 'filters', 'mosaic' and 'classification'.

4. From preliminary archaeological observations the visible upper part of Drupad Kilā reasonably spans the second half of the first millennium BC and first century AD.

2

Kāmpilya: One Site or More Sites?

Annamaria Dallaporta
Lucio Marcato

THE question posed by the title is the first reason for the research which began at the end of 1994, in collaboration, from the very first mission to the site of Kāmpil, with the Kanpur Pāñcāla Institute. Since then two more surveys have been made with the aim of determining a possible spatial and temporal context to our question. A first relation, between what resulted and what was then focused, is the subject of our notes.

Archaeological Antecedents: An Outline

The village of Kāmpil, lat. 27°36'N, long. 79°17'E, is situated in the district of Farrukhābād, *tahsīl* of Kāimgañj (Uttar Pradesh), at about 45 km to the north-west of Fatehgarh (*fig.*1). It is a typical agricultural village of the Ganges plain, in the fertile territory of Doāb between Ganges and Yamunā rivers, whose present aspect gives the idea of concealing a past is of great interest.

Kāmpil was identified with Kāmpilya, the capital of the ancient kingdom of South Pāñcāla (*fig.* 2), by A. Cunningham, who first visited the site in March 1878. The most eastward mound, among those which characterised the place, was then shown to him as corresponding to the site of King Drupad's palace (Doc. 1).

Only eighty years later was Kāmpil an object of attention by archaeologists again. It appeared, in fact, in both, in one with the list of sites with Painted Grey Ware (PGW) and in the other with Northern Black Polished Ware (NBPW), made by B.B. Lal in 1954-5.[1] The first list shows a rough topographical mistake,

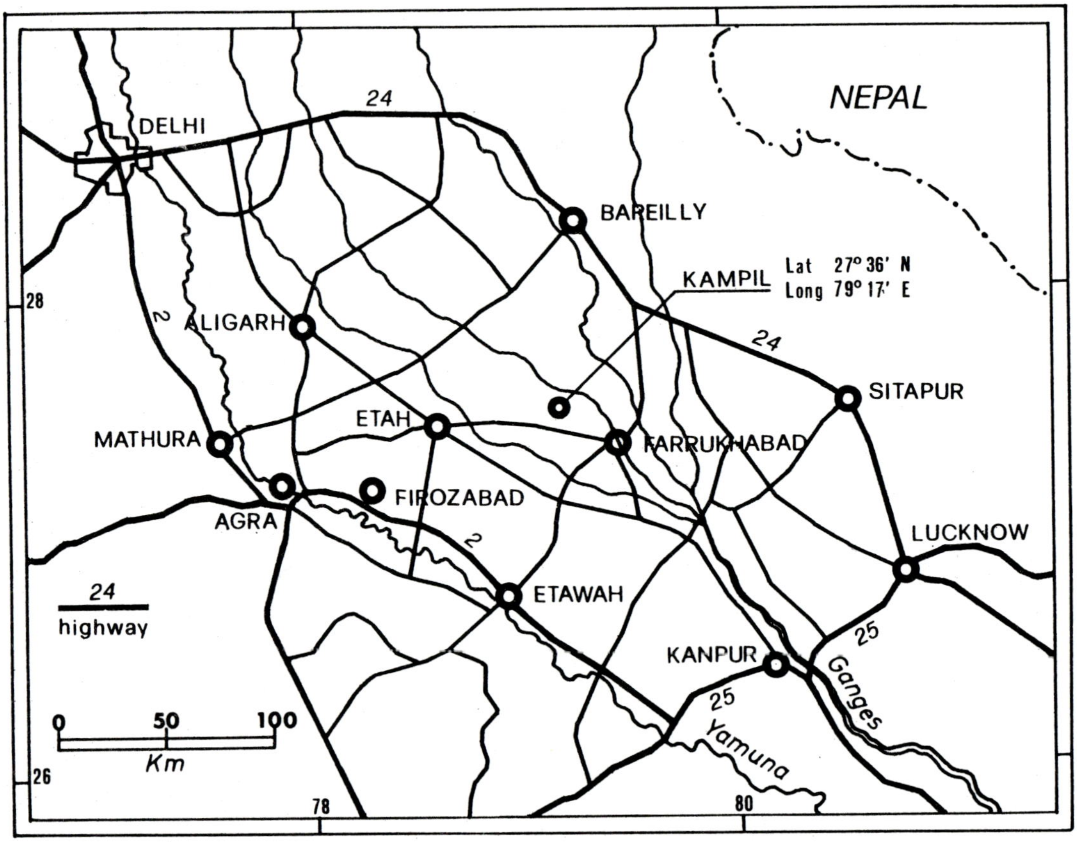

↑ *fig.* 1 : Schematic portion of the road map indicating the village of Kāmpil.

already found in Nando Lal Dey (1927, p. 88), according to which Kāmpil would be located 28 miles north-east of Fatehgarh, in the district of Farrukhābād, instead of lying towards north-west.

The first official survey dates back to 1961. It was made by V.N. Misra of Deccan College Postgraduate and Research Institute, Poona. He confirmed the identity of the present village with Kāmpilya; he identified the mound, about 5 m high, situated on north-western side of the settlement,[2] locally known as Draupadigarh; he recognised the presence of PGW, a small quantity of NBPW and medieval glazed pottery. On that occasion an engraved terracotta disk was found.

In 1976 K.K. Sinha of Department of Ancient Indian History, Culture and Archaeology, Banaras Hindu University, dug six trenches at Kāmpil, with the aim of defining borders of the settlement where PGW was used. Excavations[3] showed that the

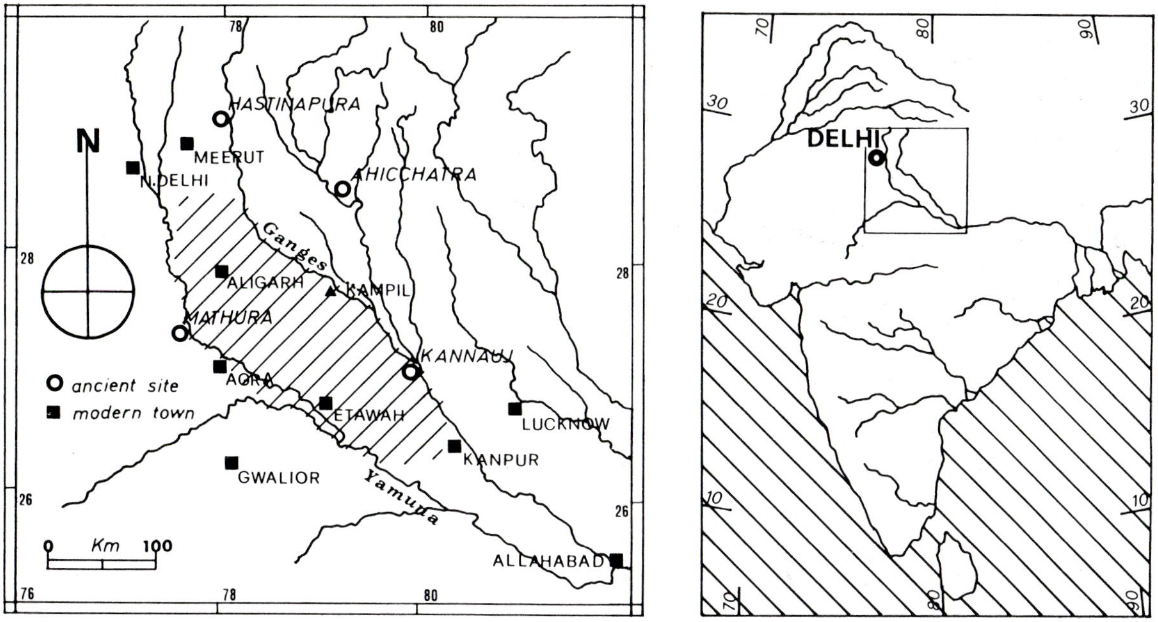

↑ *fig.* 2 : The cross-hatched area (mostly contained between the Ganges and Yamunā rivers) indicates the territory of the ancient kingdom of South Pāñcāla.

deposit of PGW 2.40 m thick[4] lay on natural soil together with fine grey ware, Black Slipped Ware (BSW) and Black and Red Ware (BRW). Overlying layers belonged to late medieval period. Also a clay embankment 1.70 m high, whose base width could not be ascertained, was then noticed. Some sculptures were recovered from medieval layers.

In the same year V. Tripathi, in his work on PGW (1976, p. 140), compared the association of Kāmpil ware with the one of Hastināpura; the fact that painted potsherds were smaller in number in the former site, was explained with the place's more eastward position in the Ganges valley. According to information given by K.K. Sinha himself, several terracotta objects were found during the excavation: disks both plain and decorated, conic plugs, animal figurines, beads and small balls together with copper needles and other objects.

T.N. Roy (1986, pp. 51-2), who collaborated to K.K. Sinha's research, offers more detailed information and gives a first interpretation of the resulting data: the ancient inhabitants of Kāmpil were residing on the bank of the river Ganges, which now flows 3 km farther off. The mound upon which part of the present village is built, had an extension of about 1 km. Six trenches dug out in 1976, integrated with twelve exposed sections, had revealed that the level of the natural soil was comparatively uniform. It was lowered, however, by about 3 m from the centre of the mound towards north/north-west, probably because of erosion by the river in remote times. Together with PGW there were red ware, fine grey ware, BSW and BRW, as were already noticed in other sites with PGW deposits. The presence of samples of NBP ware showed that the site belonged to late PGW period, corresponding to the period of *janapada* in the middle of the Iron Age. Moreover, the lack of a separate deposit of BRW beneath the PGW layer suggests absence from the place of first period of the Iron Age. Nor was there any evidence of the late Iron Age.

These observations made on the basis of data derived from investigations done on the spot and official excavations, are however only very concisely related, while descriptions of archaeological remains visible on the surface lack in documentation.

From G.B. Singh (1979, pp. 36-7) and Meenu Gupta (1992) we learn that terracotta figurines found on the occasion may be ascribed to a period between second century BC and first century AD. The vitality of the place, though not always at the same level, stretched until Mughal times.

At Kāmpil, scattered in the present village, there can be seen also numerous architectonic stone remains, such as door-posts, architraves, etc., either engraved and decorated or simply squared, which can be attributed to eighth-tenth centuries AD.[5]

The state museum of Lucknow preserves some of the most significant stone sculptures, more or less damaged, and terracotta figurines found on the site on several occasions.

Data gathered up to now on Kāmpil history and in particular results of the excavation made in 1976, indicate the beginning of human presence in the place not earlier than seventh century BC, which seem however to deny Cunningham's hypothesis. In that case we should assume the existence of a site only occasionally inhabited before the appearance of a stable population mainly characterised by PGW production, whose continual presence is witnessed by a large amount of fine ware and an archaeological layer about two metres deep. Ancient literature, however, dates Kāmpilya further back in time, and gives it an importance to a royal dignity which clearly contrasts with results of 1976 excavation.

Kāmpilya, besides being a prosperous town, was also an important Jaina and Buddhist religious centre. Tradition in fact recognises the town as the birth place of thirteenth *tīrthaṅkara* Vimalanātha. Translating *tīrthāṅkara* with "pontifex",[6] we can suppose the place to have been strictly connected with the river Ganges and perhaps have been the site of a particularly strategic ford. To underline the importance of the town, moreover, there is proof of its connection with most importantly inhabited centres of the period. The 'Grand Route' from Taxilā led to Vaiśālī and farther, at Pānīpat divided into two branches: the southern one went also through Kāmpilya (*fig.* 3). This road, about seven to eight metres wide, was not an alternative to the waterway but rather complementary to it, connecting far off places lying on banks of different rivers. Probably routes winding along plains were marked out, among slight undulations of ground, following the long natural levees,[7] whose surface was adequately adapted.

fig. 3 : A hypothetical plotting of a part of two branches (N and S) of the Grand Route. Circles indicate ancient sites, while squares indicate modern cities. Broken lines indicate a number of connection links and other roads. ↓

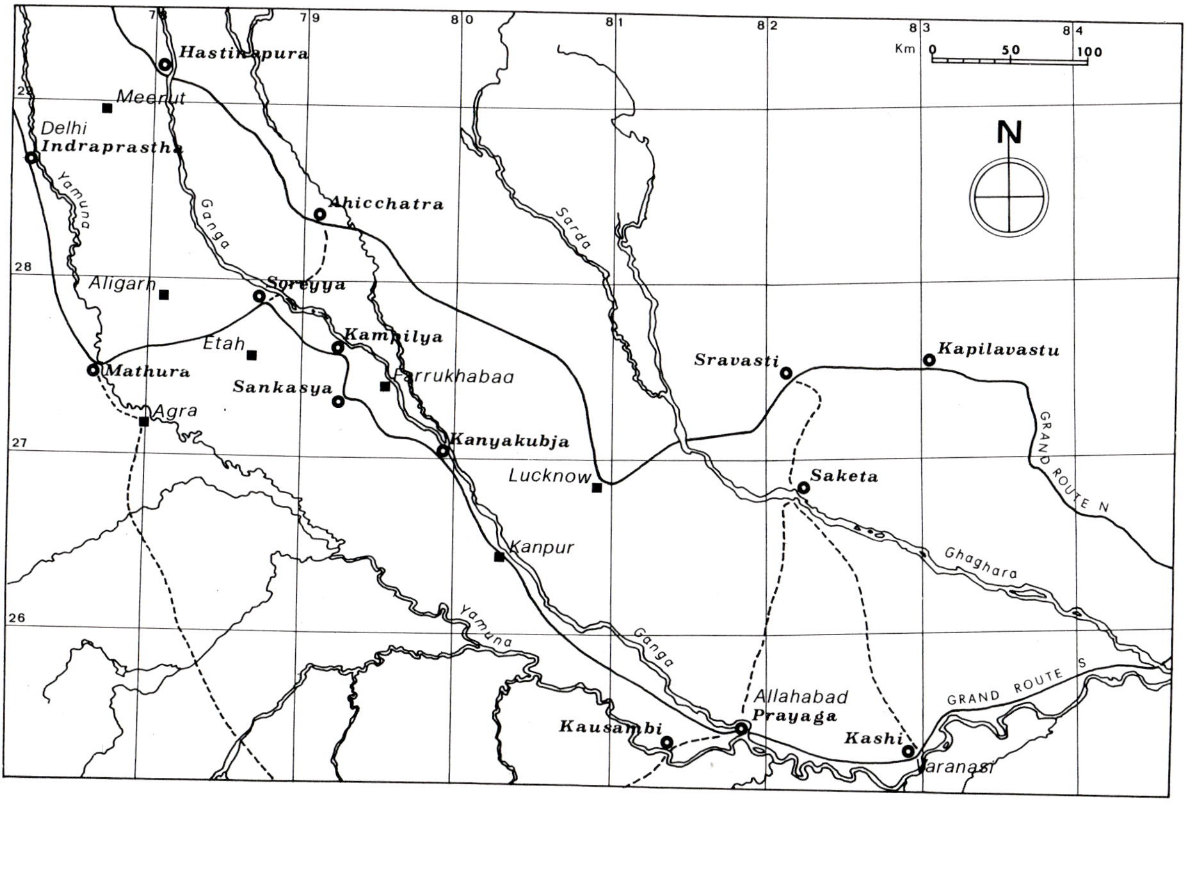

The coincidence, after so many centuries, of part of today's roads and railways with the ancient layout, shows that choices[8] made in past are still valid from a functional point of view.

Limited archaeological researches carried out at Kāmpil up to now cannot be considered definitive, therefore the identity of Kāmpil-Kāmpilya has still to be proved: the extension of the most ancient site may, only in part, have coincided with the settlement area characterised by PGW, investigated in 1976. The spatial distribution of the city may have been very articulate with permanent settlers varying both in time and space,[9] therefore a very fortunate chance could drive an almost dot-like excavation right into the heart of *Mahābhārata* Kāmpilya. As far as we know, in fact the city itself, during its long history connected with the river Ganges, may have more than once been displaced some kilometres farther off.

Moreover, we must observe that the emphasis made by some Indian archaeologists to particular ware classes, considered by them sufficient to define cultures and chronologies, is now showing all its weakness. Similar uses of archaeological records have for long years conditioned researches leading to over-simplified conclusions, which must therefore be considered with suspicion.

Bearing all this in mind, between 1996 and 1997 we investigated Kāmpil territory, aiming to define the palaeo-ambient frame around Kāmpil (about 10 km) with particular regards to hydrological situations on which settlements' rise and fortunes depended.

The Geoarchaeological Study: Some Notes

The flatland of Doāb slopes gently from north-west to south-east, following the predominant direction of the river Ganges, with almost constant uniformity, interrupting only at intervals by slight and seemingly insignificant undulations.

As a matter of fact, these slight variations of height represent the remains of ambient modifications whose evolution in time has been highlighted by a geomorphological research made on an area of about 3,000 km. The study was carried on with help of remote sensing techniques,[10] based on the use of multispectral images cast by LISS sensor of the Indian satellite IRS-1B (IRS. L

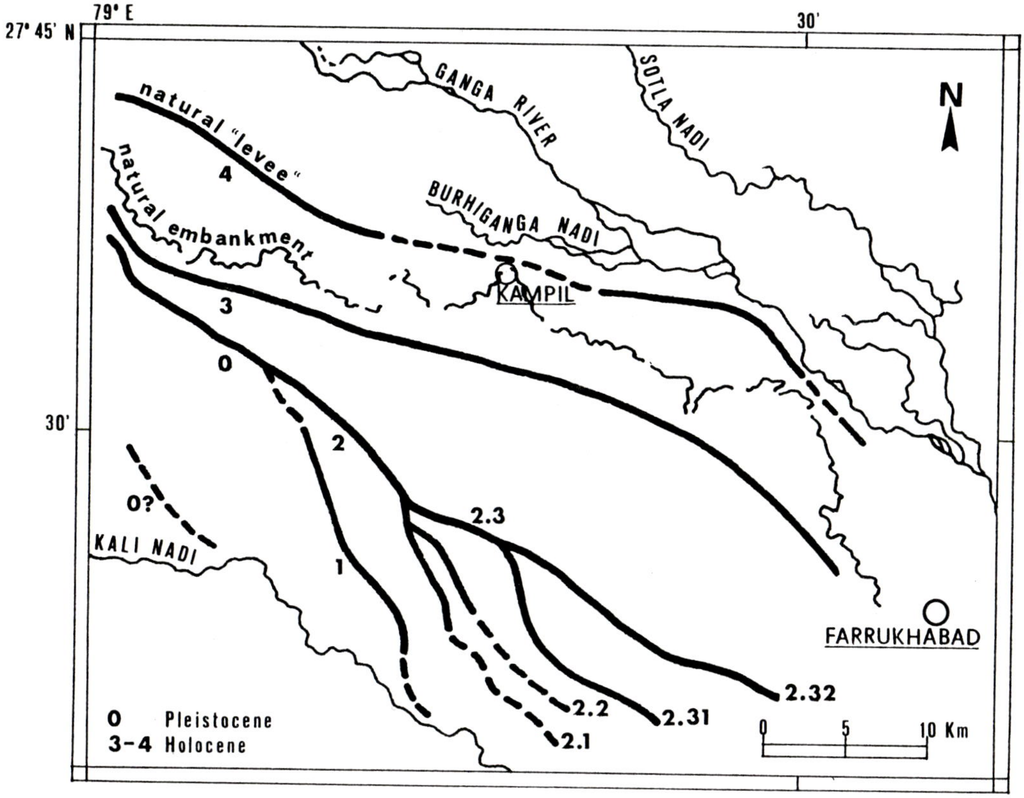

↑
fig. 4 : A summary of evolutions of natural levees along ancient riverbeds of the Ganges. The indented embankment of the late Holocene river terrace is visible between Points 3 and 4.

II-B 2.27.48 e IRS. L II-A 2.27.48), cartographic means, applicative GIS systems, and surveys on the field. It was therefore possible to verify the entity of shifting of the Ganges water-course from south-west to north-east. This shifting was however already known and is still in progress. Ancient riverbeds are now represented by a series of natural levees (fluvial watersheds) directed from north-west to south-east, which may be grouped into two classes differing both in typology and area (*fig.* 4): one to north with simple and almost parallel reliefs (n. 3 and n. 4), and the other to south in which an important levee opens in a fan-like structure comprising a series of smaller levees (n. 1; n. 2; n. 2.1; n. 2.2; n. 2.3; n. 2.3.1; n. 2.3.2). The comparison with similar palaeographic elements and morphofluvial dynamics enables us to recognise, in this context of landscape shapes, traces of two genetic phases: one probably belonging to Pleistocene (the southerner part), and the other belonging to Holocene (the northerner part). Watersheds of subsequent water-courses which roughly skirt today's alluvial plains of Ganges and whose sloping corresponds to the general sloping of the Ganges plain itself, are results of river's sedimentation during the Quaternary age. They show different alternating periods of natural bank building and overflowing.

By comparing and superimposing these cartographic elements over prints of two multi-spectral images, we were able to study the connection between the morphology of the soil and types of soil highlighted by different brightnesses. We generally find a sandy, more saline, and therefore less fertile soil in the area characterised by more ancient watershed levees than in the northerner area characterised by thick and intensive cultivation, typical of more fertile clay and slimy soil. Moreover, the considerable difference in density and in distribution of superficial waters between the Pleistocene part and the Holocene one comes out quite clearly: in the middle part, in fact, corresponding to Holocene depositing phase, water net is much thicker than in the southern part which is more ancient.

In late Holocene protohistoric times intense activity of Ganges brought to the formation of an extended and continuous river terrace delimited by an embankment of few metres difference in level, which corroded northern side of the most recent natural levee. Along this natural boundary line of today's alluvial plain there are several villages. Kāmpil is one of them. For its closeness to the river, the morphologic firmness of the ground sheltered from floods and possibly the presence of a ford have played a determining role in the choice for establishing a settlement there.

These considerations brought us to survey the small embankment upstream and downstream of Kāmpil for about 10 km, leading to the identification of a particularly interesting settlement besides other minor sites of different ages.

DRUPAD KILĀ

The located site (lat. 27°36'13"N — long. 79°12'30"E) spreads over 900,000 m^2, expanded around a rectangular shaped settlement, locally called Drupad Kilā. The settlement is enclosed by a wall along which there are also some evident upstanding tracts. The sides of the rectangle measures 780 m and 660 m, and the longest is oriented east to west (*fig.* 5a; *fig.* 5b).

Other cities were constructed with quadrangular layout in

other times in India. Due to its striking resemblance to Drupad Kilā, we cite the Harappan city of Dholavira recently unearthed by R.S. Bisht after excavations began in 1989.

The rectangular shape of the city wall, it's dimensions, orientation of it's sides, and the off-centre position of gates are all similar to same elements in Drupad Kilā, and provide layouts of two cities with the same shape (*fig.* 6).

The Settlement

In Pāñcāla, as in rest of India, first post-Harappan fortifications with unbaked bricks were built about seventh-sixth century BC,[11] while baked brick walls for defence (at first only in the facing) were used later starting from the Maurya age.

The defence wall must have been preceded by a moat external to the regular perimeter of the settlement. In *Arthaśāstra* digging of three moats are recommended with decreasing length and depth. The clay derived from them had to be used both for levelling city's ground, and, duly tamped, for building the basement for the wall itself. Inside the settlement, parallel to this city wall, there ran a road (*ghaṇṭā-mārga*, in *Samarāṅgaṇa-sūtradhāra*, 10. 16[12]) similar to a Roman *pomerium* (*fig.* 7). At a

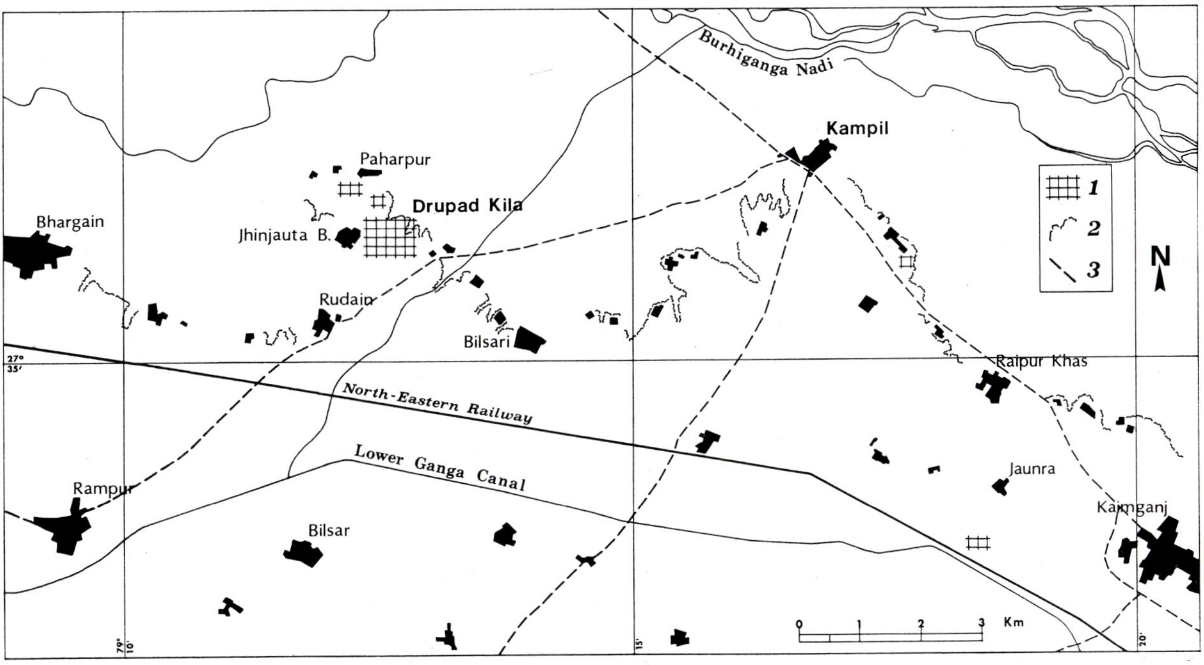

fig. 5a : The location of Drupad Kilā and other sites discovered: 1. Ancient site; 2. Natural embankment; 3. Main road. ↓

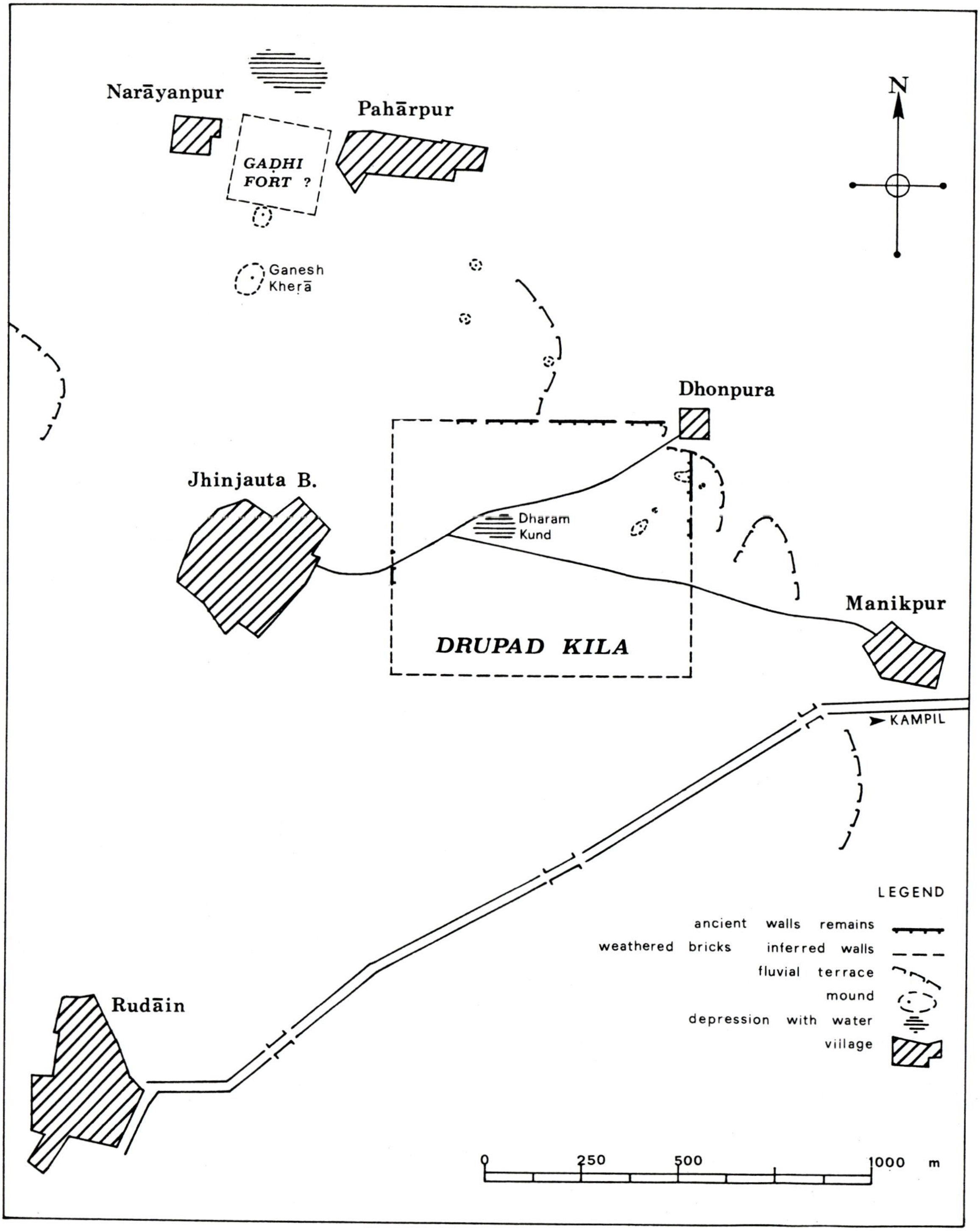

Narāyanpur
Pahārpur
GADHI FORT ?
Ganesh Kherā
N
Dhonpura
Jhinjauta B.
Dharam Kund
Manikpur
DRUPAD KILA
KAMPIL
LEGEND
ancient walls remains
weathered bricks inferred walls
fluvial terrace
mound
depression with water
village
Rudāin
0 250 500 1000 m

← *fig.* 5b : The layout of the ancient settlement of Drupad Kilā.

regular distance on the sides and in the corners, there could be built some towers, which *Arthaśāstra* recommends to be provided with a balustrade (probably battlemented in Maurya period, at least, as far as it can be inferred by Sāñcī reliefs). One or three doors opened on each side in correspondence to principal roads' axes.

Actually, there are some differences both in building techniques and in materials used: a wall could be built with 'boxes' filled with clay and gravel[13] or with superimposed steps perhaps made homogeneous and smoothed with clay.[14] When the wall is all built in baked bricks, moats built normally among the three indicated, may be absent.

There are different opinions about the function of the first embankment-walls: a wall represents for certain a very drastic and functional separation between the inside and the outside somehow felt as unsafe and threatening. They believed that the threat should come (at least at first) either from the river close to the town, then considered as an enemy, or from a real enemy (from third-second century BC onwards), is by now irrelevant. Of course, such a separation qualified the inner ground giving it also a symbolic meaning, which may explain the presence of

fig. 6 : Schematic layout of Dholavira. 1. Lower town; 2. Medium town; 3. Citadel. ↘

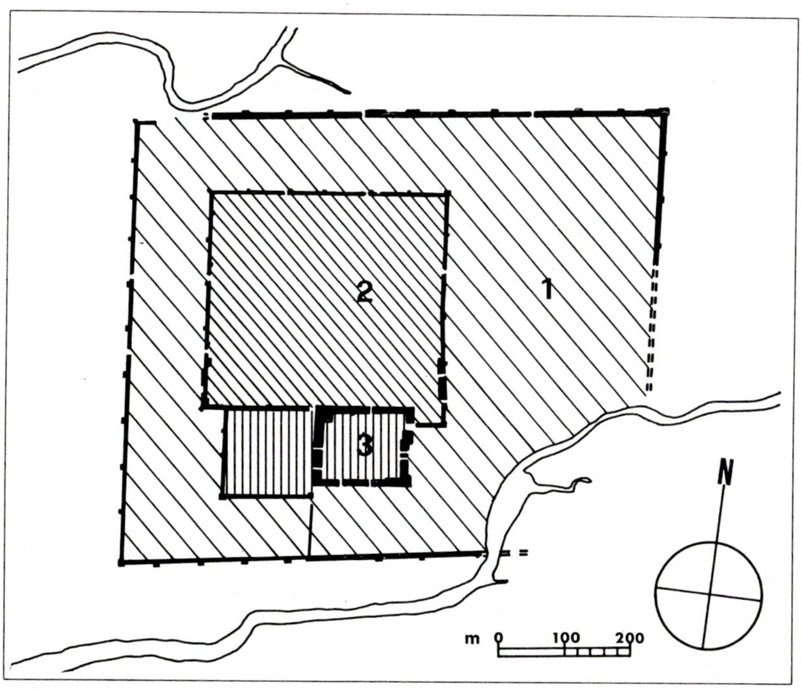

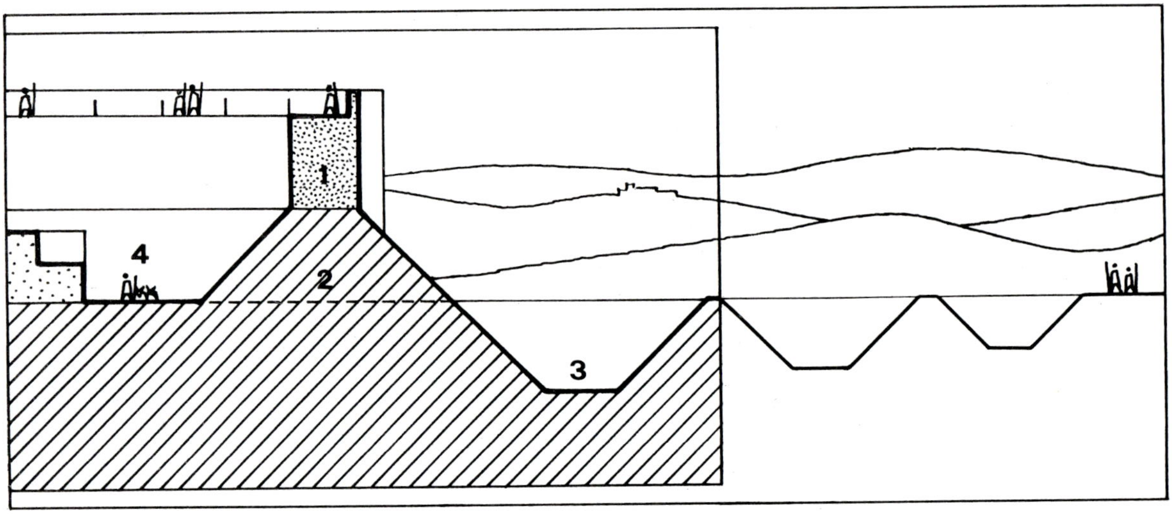

walls too thin for defence.

↑ *fig.* 7 : Diagrammatic section of city fortifications, by Arthaśāstra. The insert indicates the situation most usually observed in unearthed cities.
1. Prākāra; 2. Vapra; 3. Patikhā; 4. Ghaṇṭā-mārga.

The Drupad Kilā wall, whose average width in its visible tracks is about 350 cm (with a maximum of about 500 cm), was built with baked bricks, upon a similar pre-existing lower mud structure (*fig.* 8). There are no traces either of towers or ramparts at regular intervals. A wall head (western side), some gaps in the structural continuity and varied thickness of the wall (northern side) suggest the existence of wall doors. There are no wall tracks at the north-eastern corner for about 100 m in both directions, perhaps due to erosion, collapse, or removal caused by ruinous floods and man's action. The size of wall bricks (30/40×21/25×45/55 cm) dates this construction around second half of the Early Historic Period (second century BC-fourth century AD).[15]

Size and Shape of the Town

A town with a surface of 50 ha existing about the end of the first millennium BC in Doāb, was a rather important settlement, though perhaps not important enough to become a capital under 'normal' conditions. In fact, the place where the king and his court resided differed highly from other settlements, both as regards extension and quality. The capital was up to ten times larger than most important towns and besides services, its

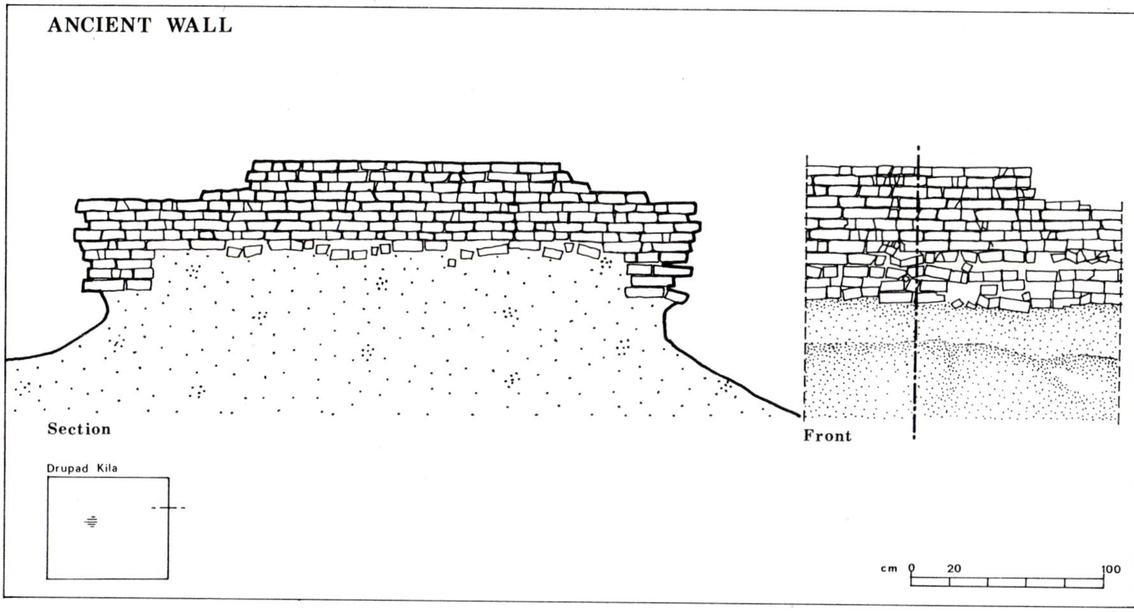

↑ *fig.* 8 : Section and front view of a part of the wall surrounding Drupad Kilā. The wall was built with burnt bricks above a clay embankment. Bricks of which only a few courses remain are tightly cemented using mortar.

cultural, social and economical (sometimes even religious) opportunities were markedly superior to those offered by any other town in the kingdom. The concentration of many symbolic spaces, as represented by a capital, had to be very well characterised in order absolutely not to be confused with other towns, according to parameters immediately perceptible. This at least seems to be the reality derived from archaeological records and from literature, though not always in total agreement.

Therefore, on comparing the surface inside Drupad Kilā walls to one of other capitals (between second century BC and second century AD) a great disparity is evident (e.g.: Ahicchatra 180 ha; Śrāvastī 160 ha; Kauśāmbī 160 ha; Mathurā 295 ha) (*fig*.9). Drupad Kilā may therefore be considered to have been a big town in Pāñcāla, as important as Atrañjikhera, but it being practically unknown and unmentioned in ancient literature (at least as far as we know as yet), it seems very strange and leads to different hypotheses which can be set aside in absence of sufficient archaeological data.

The regularity of the settlement's shape suggests a precise planning, in accordance with canonical directions. However if the shape of a town is the result of different and even partly contrasting requirements, after so many centuries, the underlying demands, adjustments, compromises, etc., will be found out only in part. In our case, anyhow, both, the rectangle with major axis east to west, and the northern side next to the right bank of the river, are in accordance with tradition, though the building practice of the time generally seemed to overlook the treatises' rules and proportions.

As far as we know today, during the period under examination only Kaliṅganagara or Toṣali (Śiśupālgarh, Bhubaneśvar district, Orissa) had a more or less regular planimetry, but was larger in size than Drupad Kilā (140 ha)[16] and differently orientated.

The settlement's surface is about 6 m above the ground level in northern part, while to south the difference in height is almost nil, due to elevation of the surrounding land. Inside Drupad Kilā the inhabited area was prevalently built with unbaked bricks. Some regular furrowings are probably evidences of ancient roads.

fig. 9 : A comparison of shapes and sizes between a few of most important fortified urban centres (second Century BC – second century AD) and Drupad Kilā. ↓

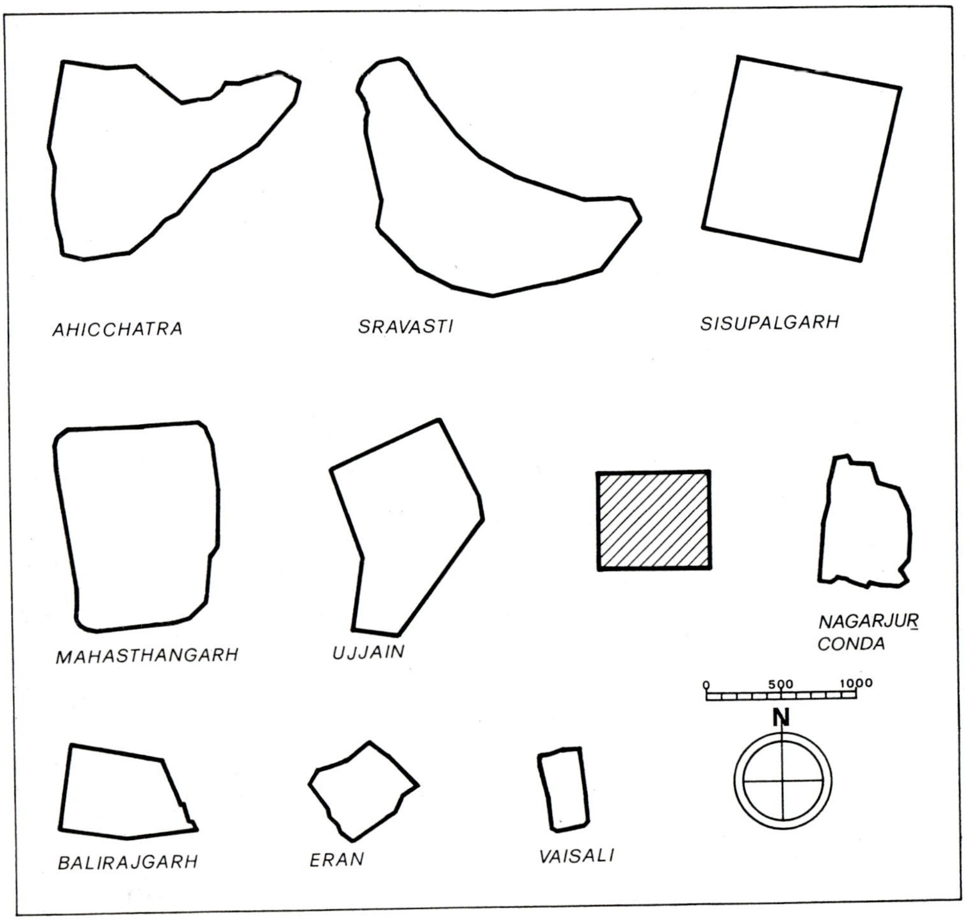

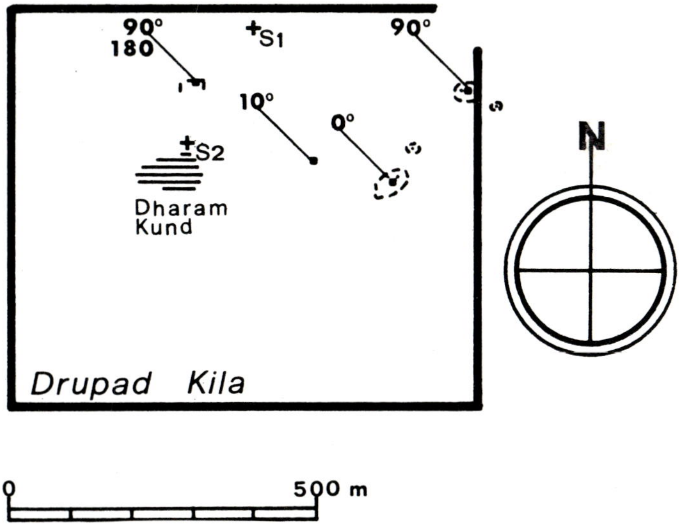

↑ *fig.* 10a : Inside Drupad Kilā: natural exposed sections S1 and S2 and some courses of brick on the place (the numbers refer to the orientation of courses).

On some small mounds to the east, a few remains of baked brick buildings, not well identified as yet, have been singled out.

Archaeological Observations

Some exposed and surveyed sections (*fig.* 10a) have evidenced large waste pits with layers of ash and sherds (*fig.* 10b; *fig.* 10c). In one of them, there were numerous animal bones mixed with ash in a layer of at least 10 cm. Pits, approximately 50 cm deep, open just under the ground surface and rest on a thick layer (up to 150 cm) of sandy clay. The absence of any deposit over pits' surfaces may be due both to erosion and levelling and ploughing of the soil for agricultural purposes.

Before a systematic survey is carried out, we can report some observations.

The area of Drupad Kilā is abundant with scatters of plenty of sherds especially in northern part. Two well-known ware classes are absent: PGW and NBPW. Only some red ware sherds with moulded decorations (*Ill. 1*) were found which could date back to a period between seventh and fourth centuries BC.[17] For the moment, however, considering, the persistence of some ware kinds over time, prevalence of certain later classes, and absence of stratigraphical study, it seems more convenient to date the ware from about second century BC, as for other well-known sites in U. P. Red ware is found in common shapes that prevailed in former centuries: bowls, vases, jars, dishes, *hāṇḍīs*, lids (*fig.* 11). Bottle-necked vases and spouted vases prove the vitality of this site in the last phase of the Early Historical Period (second to fourth century AD) (*fig.* 12). Less frequent are sherds of polished red ware, decorated with horizontal black lines (*Ill.* 2), and mica dust slipped red ware leading to the classical phase of Late Historical Period (fourth to seventh century AD). Though in a very small number, there are also some red wares with relief

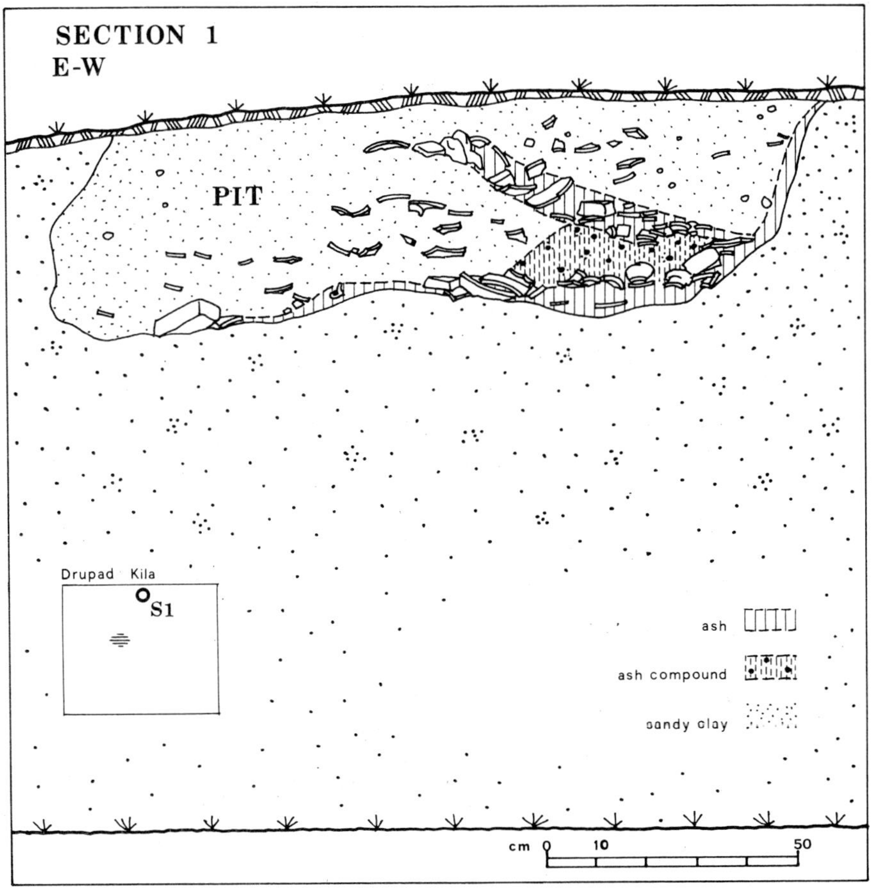
SECTION 1
E-W
PIT
Drupad Kila
S1
ash
ash compound
sandy clay
cm 0 10 50

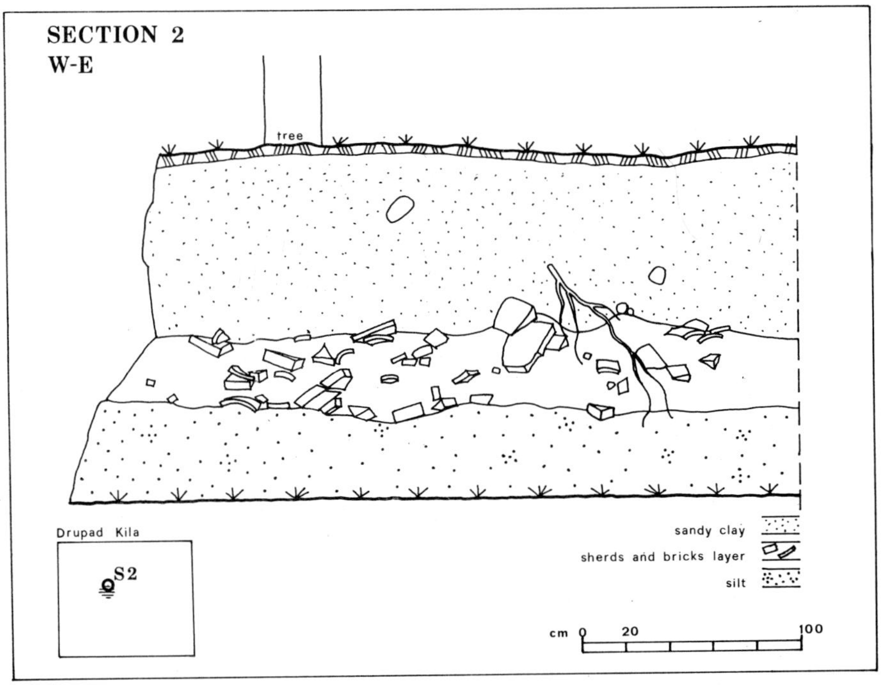
SECTION 2
W-E
tree
Drupad Kila
S2
sandy clay
sherds and bricks layer
silt
cm 0 20 100

←

fig. 10b : Section 1: this refers to what was probably a pit. Only pit's most evident throws are shown.

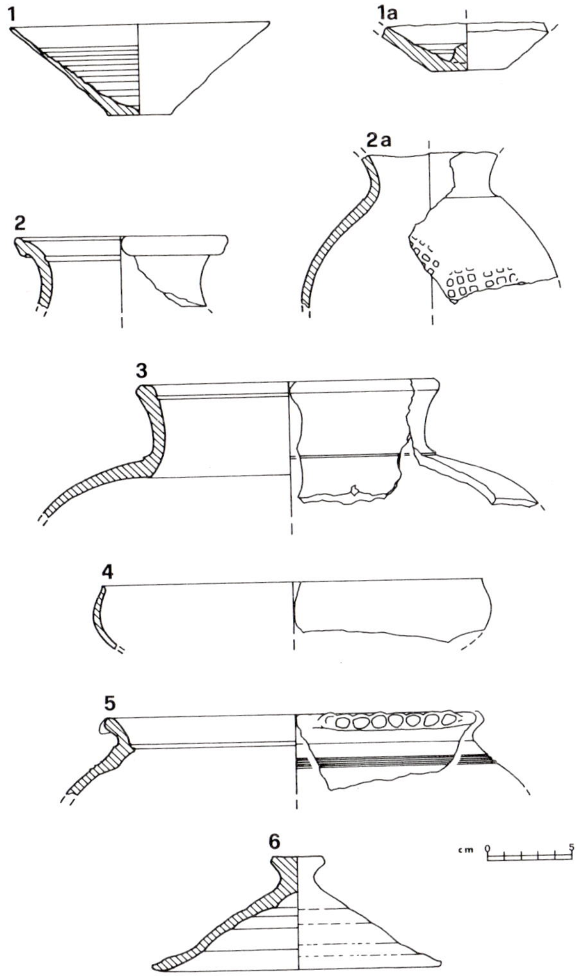

←

fig. 10c : Section 2: This is found on north bank of Dharam Kūnd and shows it a deposit of fictile material laid down chaotically.

↑

fig. 11 : Red Ware from the surface: sherds of: 1. Bowl; 1a. Bowl with central knob; 2. Vase; 2a. Jar with printed grid decoration; 3. Jar; 4. Dish; 5. *Hāṇḍī*; 6. Lid.

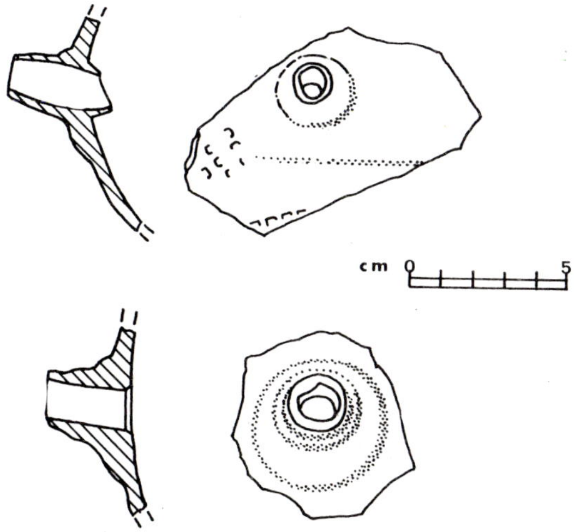

→

fig. 12 : Red Ware from the surface: necks of spouted vases.

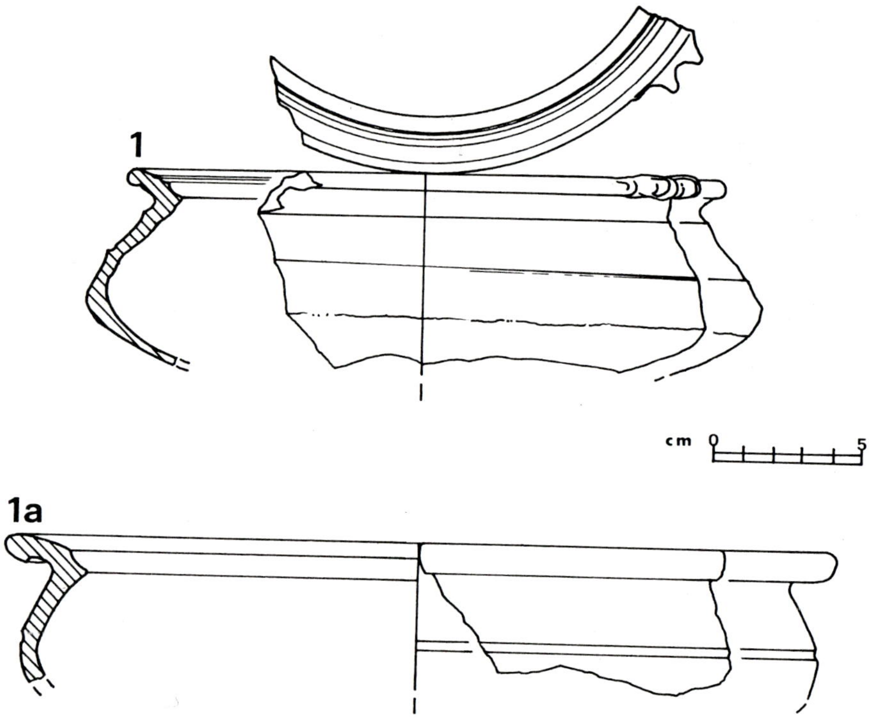

decoration, whose characteristics can be referred to pre-Gupta and Gupta periods (*Ill.* 3). The grey ware is also abundantly documented in the same shape as the red ware (*fig.* 13). Moreover, many roughly disk-like shaped and differently sized potsherds — called 'hopscotches' by Indian archaeologists — have been found. They can be dated to second half of the Early Historical Period (*Ill.* 4).

Two fragments of clay architectonic decoration, both with rectangular and volute reliefs, might come from religious buildings of the Gupta period (*fig.* 14).

Framed *kaṅkar* slabs, some regular decorative elements, and a sandstone relief with the central figure of Sarasvatī flanked by two attendants, substantiate the presence of temples between ninth and eleventh centuries AD (*Ill.* 5).

Several wall tracks made of baked bricks of the same size as those of the city wall, suggest that important buildings were erected with plundering material either at the same time of the wall's or in the subsequent period (*fig.* 10a).

↑
fig. 13 : Grey Ware taken from the surface; sherds of: 1. Carenated *hāṇḍī*; 2. *Hāṇḍī*.

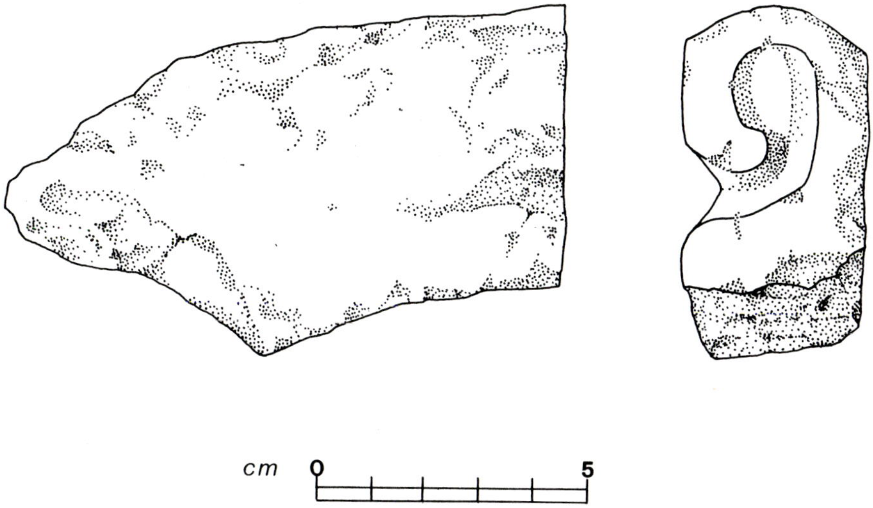

Inside the perimeter were also found some over-burnt clay slags probably belonging to walls of a kiln. The use of a very expensive structure like a kiln for pottery, may prove that there was great demand either for pottery articles, or for high quality objects. The small kilns (*gajaput*) generally used in villages from the ancient to modern times, in fact, involved a very simple baking technique which did not allow any control over the final quality of the product. It is now difficult to state when the kiln was in use. We can only say that kiln slags and demolition materials were abundantly used both as refill and building material, and were carried even very far away from their original places.

In the north-east quadrant of Drupad Kilā, shapes of two small mounds may be discerned. They will be referred to as mound A and mound B.

Mound A is aligned perpendicularly to the remains of a portion of the city wall with an almost regular shape (*fig.* 15) elongated from east to west. The greater axis is about 40 m long, while the lesser axis is about 30 m long (all measurements are estimates). The slope of the mound is not very pronounced, and in some places presents abrupt, terrace-like interruptions. The top of the mound is 4-4.5 m above the lower surrounding soil. In southern part, at a height of about 3 m from the soil, a number of lines of laid up bricks (three or more) may be seen running east to west, and at the same level all around the mound other lines of fragmented bricks without specific orientation may

↑
fig. 14 : Fragment of fictile decoration in rectangular scroll shape.

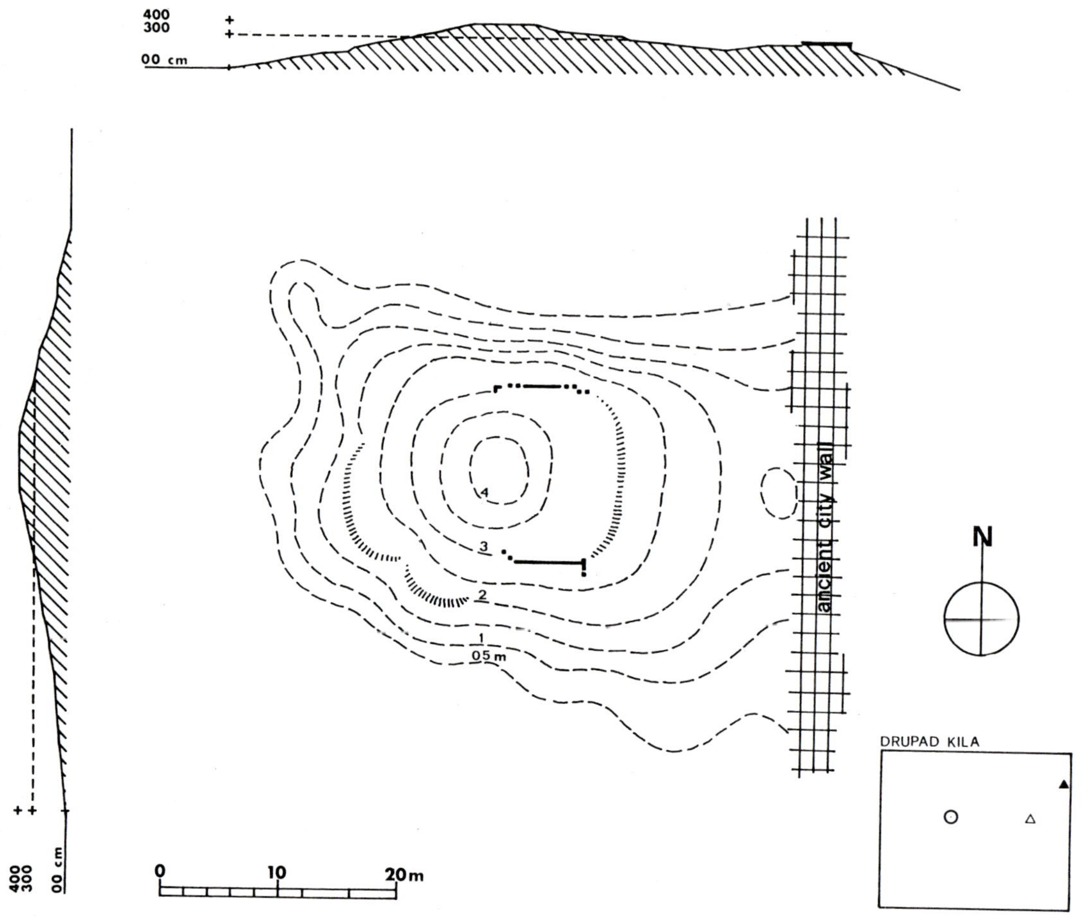

also be seen. This leads us to suppose for the existence of a platform. The remains on observation seem to indicate that the structure occupied nearly mound's entire area and had a square shape of 15 m dimension. The structure is now eroded and has collapsed on western side, where the slope of the mound is greatest (*fig.* 16).

The shape of the mound presents a second smaller top to the east immediately near Drupad Kilā wall.

The surface of the mound presents numerous sherds of grey and red ware, in addition to a few small cone-shaped fragments and curved bricks of 10 × 7 cm dimension.

Mound B is more regular in shape than mound A, which presents similar measurements and is elongated in south-east

↑ *fig.* 15 : A sketch of the layout and contours of mound A.

to north-west direction (*fig.* 17). In this mound as well, there appears to have been a construction, demonstrated by the presence of six and more layers of brick, which originally must have occupied nearly mound's entire area. The small part of horizontal surface in brick that can be seen towards north presents a decidedly marked curvature, which in this case makes the supposition of a platform more problematical. Although layers of bricks may be discerned, but directional alignment of these courses of bricks cannot be established with certainty.

In addition to numerous sherds, the surface provides a thin curved section of terracotta (perhaps from a building), fragments of small common objects, and the 'relic' shown in *fig.* 22.

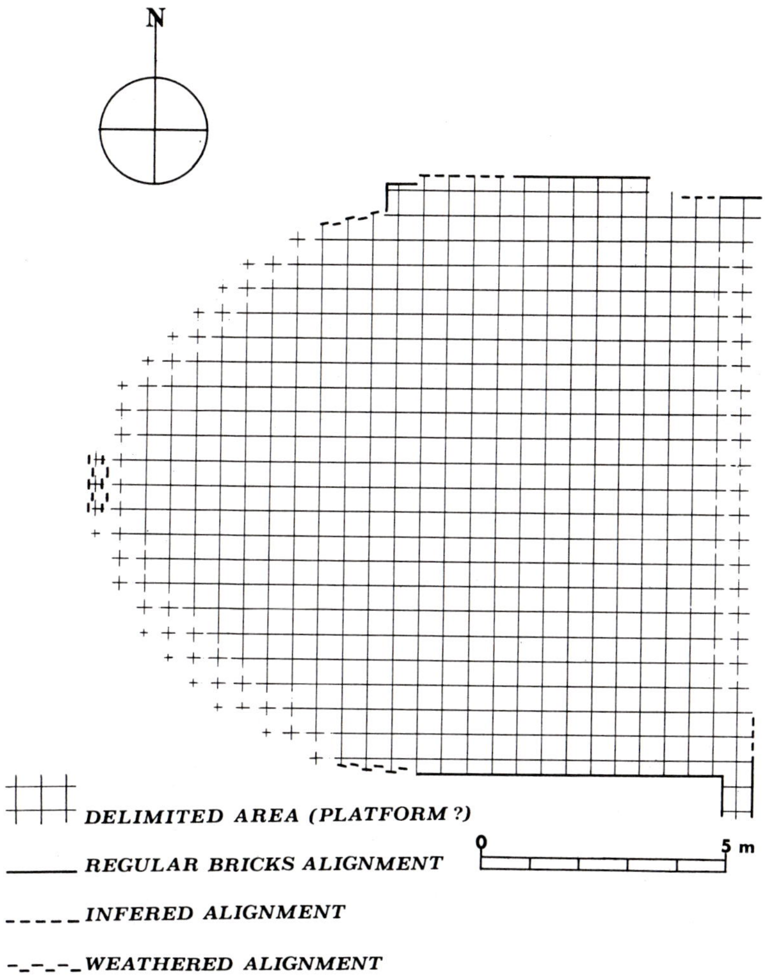

→ *fig.* 16 : Drawing of remains of what was probably the platform in mound A.

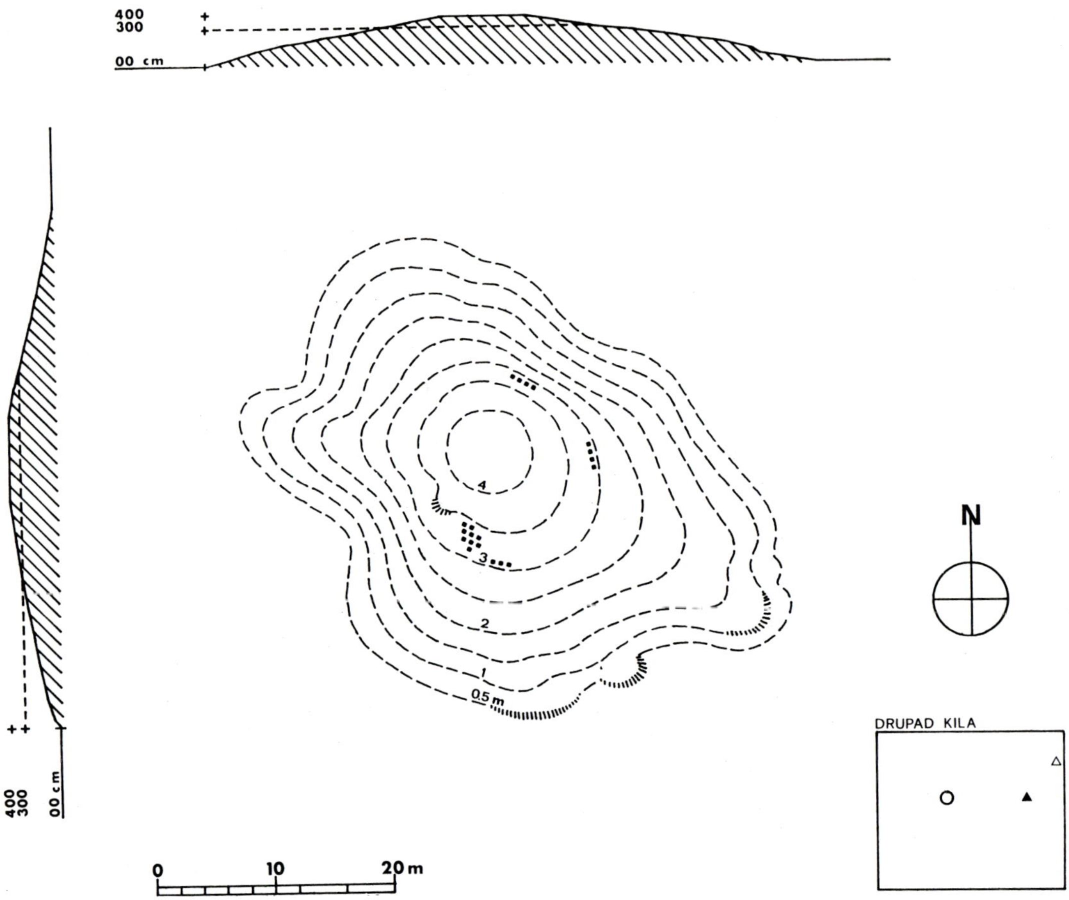

In both mounds, brick structures rest on a layer of clay about 3 m high. This might have been an embankment constructed expressly to provide a raised base for possible higher structures. The height might have been increased by erosion at the foot of the embankment.

Slightly farther to the west (about 50 m) of mound B, a number of exposed portions of over-burnt clay surface may be seen, which if hypothetically assembled together might have covered an area of 8-10 m^2. Isolated by evident erosive action, these surfaces lie 70-100 cm below the nearest ground level.

The limited surface area of the zone in question may suggest the presence of artisan work performed even earlier than the time in which work of kiln, indicated by the slag from over-burnt clay found at the surface level about 150 m further south (*fig.* 18), could have existed.

↑ *fig.* 17 : A sketch of the layout and contours of mound B.

Ill. 1 : Sherds with printed decoration to which certain scholars ascribe a period that ranges from seventh century BC to fourth century AD.

Ill. 2 : Sherds of polished Red Ware decorated with horizontal black lines.

Ill. 3 : Sherds of Red Ware with relief decoration: pre-Gupta or post-Gupta period.

Ill. 4 : Hopscotches obtained from the bulge of a vase.

Ill. 5 : Decorative element in sandstone depicting Sarasvatī flanked by two attendants (ninth-eleventh centuries AD).

Ill. 6 : Objects similar to the one shown in *fig.* 19 which date back to the Roman occupation of Sardinia — Italy (Dorgali, Civil Archaeological Museum, Window No. 25).

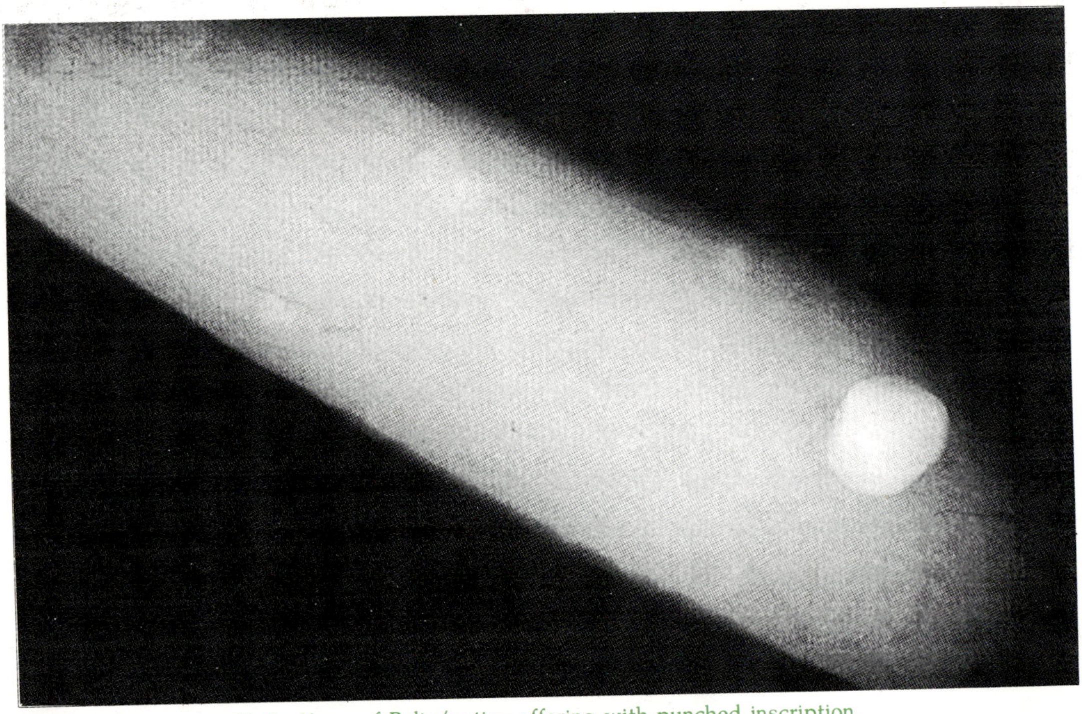

Ill. 7 : X-ray of Relic/votive offering with punched inscription.

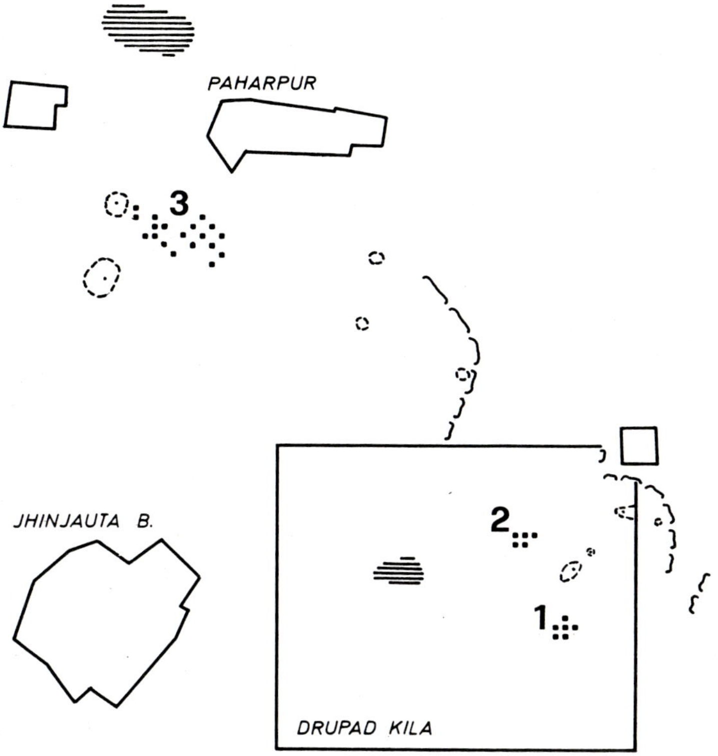

Outside the rectangular perimeter, from north to north-west, some small hillocks and mounds have been observed (*fig.* 4b). The Jhinjauta village itself, situated on a mound on the south-western side — like others — shows the same ware classes and shapes as those found on Drupad Kilā ground. Even other noted testimonies of material culture bear similar appearance in the whole settlement. Over reliefs, as well as around the area, brick fragments (4-6 cm thick) are abundant. Some *kaṅkar*-shaped and carved blocks are collected and often utilised in neighbouring villages. They may suggest presence of medieval temples.

Abundant slags (may be iron slags) are scattered by Gaṇeś Kheṛā (from east to south), but at present it is difficult to refer them to a possible metallurgic activity on the place.

Moreover, from satellite images has been derived information which coincides with collective memory of Nārāyaṇpur village, according to which a 250 m structure (Gaṛhī Fort) existed sometime in the past, north-west of Drupad Kilā, on the river bank. If the ground morphology is in agreement with all this, a corroboration concerning existence of the above-mentioned structure will only come through prospecting and diggings.

VARIOUS OBJECTS IN TERRACOTTA

There are cards below regarding a number of small objects found above soil level in the area of Drupad Kilā settlement which have been collected and stored in Kāmpil to prevent dispersion.

↑
fig. 18 : Distribution of slags: 1. Over-burnt clay slag; 2. Surface of burnt clay; 3. Metal slag.

Despite the absence of stratification context, these objects can be considered as indicators of parallelism and analogy just the same way, and also they are useful more than merely for

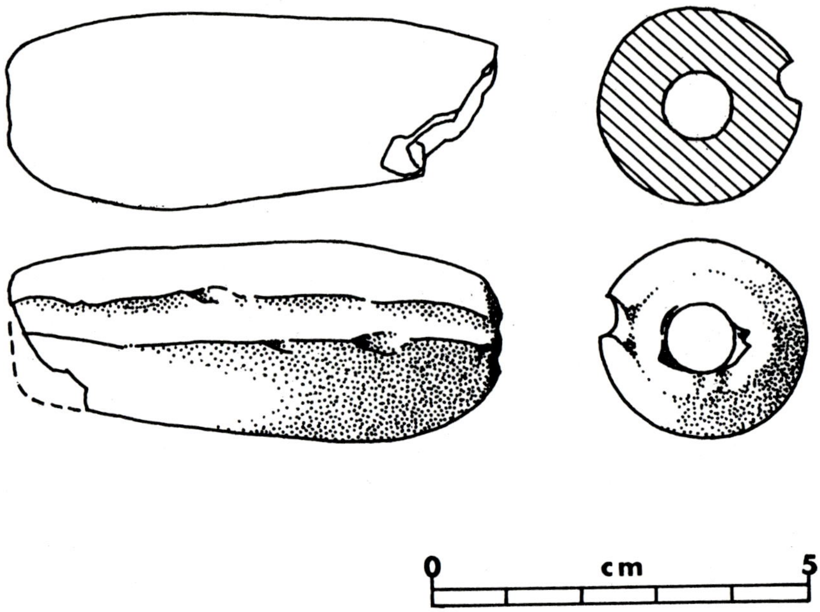

← *fig*. 19 : Cylindrical object with central hole and lateral groove.

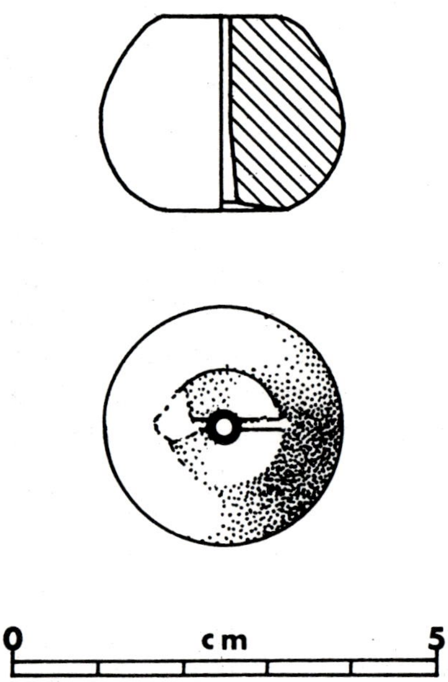

← *fig*. 20 : Spindle whorl or areca nut shaped bead.

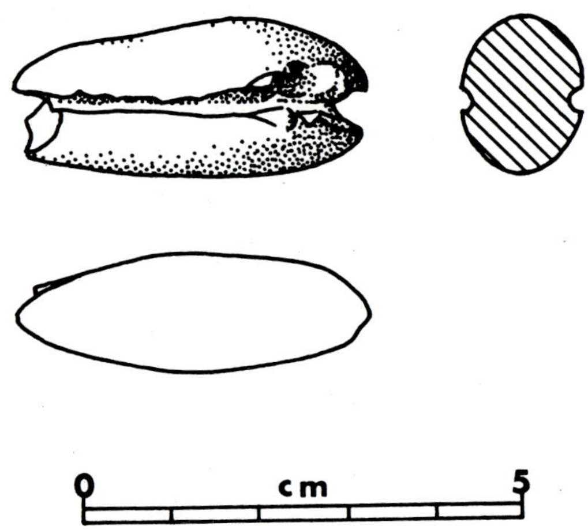

↑ *fig*. 21 : Shuttle.

systematic interpretation.

Cylinder with Central Hole (*fig.* 19)

It is an object, irregular, rounded nearly in cylindrical shape with slightly tapered ends. And it has a longitudinal groove cut without much care in almost rectilinear development.

The long hole that runs through the object has a diameter of 9 mm.

The clay mix is quite purified, as may be seen in abrasion at one end. Firing has given the object yellowish-ochre colour. The specimen was taken from an exposed section in the upper part of Jhinjhauta mound, and presumably it dates back to early Middle Age.

The use of the object is not known.

Dimensions: 65 mm in length; maximum of 26 mm in diameter.

A number of pieces of cylinders similar to the example given above, broken in transversal direction, have been found. Given their compact shape, these objects would appear more vulnerable to be crushed along its length, also due to presence of its central hole; therefore, these transversal breaks may perhaps be ascribed to the impact of its use.

Similar objects have been found in Nuraghe villages of Sardinia — Italy (Dorgali, Civil Archaeological Museum, Window No. 25) and they date back to the period of Roman occupation of the island (*Ill.* 6).

Spindle Whorl (Areca Nut-Shaped Bead) (*fig.* 20)

This twin-cone object has a crushed lower cone and a rounded surface. The concave base of the lower cone has a small, central, rectilinear groove with a hole in the middle that runs from one end of the object to the other and narrows towards the top. The chipped part of the specimen, although not very deep, reveals a clay mix quite purified. The surface of the object is smooth, and the colour is brownish-ochre.

The spindle whorl was found approximately 40 m north-west of the top of mound B.

The use of this object, of medium dimensions, was linked probably to domestic spinning activities.

Dimensions: 24 mm in height; maximum of 28 mm in diameter; cone base diameters: 14 mm (bottom cone), 12 mm (top cone); hole diameter: 4 mm at the bottom, 2 mm at the top. Many of these small objects have been found in India, and they date back to a period from the start of the Early Historical Period to the first century of modern era.

Shuttle (*fig*. 21)

This object in compressed ellipsoidal shape features a deep groove all around its longitudinal equator.

Slight chipping at one end reveals a clay mix quite purified. The surface is smooth, and the colour is reddish-brown.

The shuttle was found immediately north of the road along south-east quadrant of Drupad Kilā.

The use of objects of this shape is uncertain and in any case undocumented; its use in spinning activities appears plausible.

Dimensions: 40 mm in length; 14 mm in height; maximum of 11 mm in width.

Fragments of similar objects with different dimensions have almost throughout been found in northern part of the settlement.

Relic/Offering (*fig*. 22, a, b, and *Ill*. 7)

This object has an elongated, almost cylindrical shape that fits perfectly over three middle fingers of hand; it was made probably by rolling clay round a small inclusion of 3 or 4 mm diameter that causes the cylinder to swell out. This small inclusion (perhaps stone or bone) has a greater density than the enveloping clay, as evidenced by X-ray (performed by Dr. P.A. Singh of Lucknow). After shaping, an inscription in late Brahmi (5 mm high) was punched shallowly on the surface and it still remains to be deciphered.

The clay is quite purified and the colour is reddish-ochre.

The specimen was found at the foot of mound B (at the south-west edge).

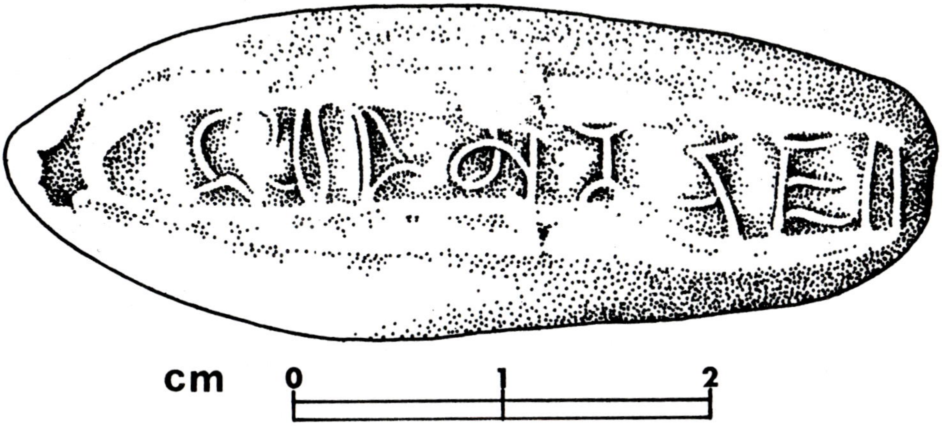

fig. 22a : Relic/votive offering with punched inscription.

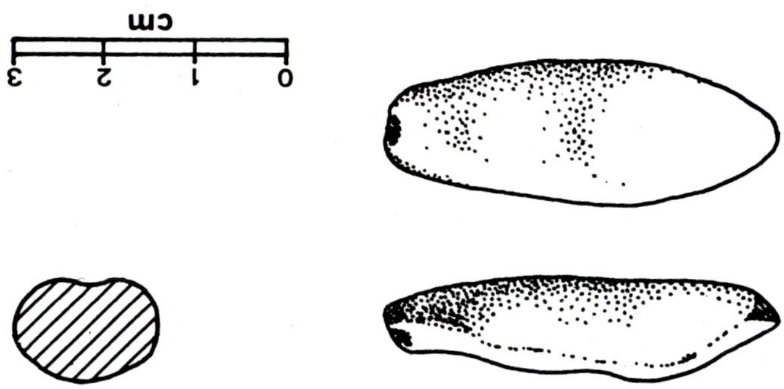

fig. 22b : Transversal section view, side and back.

This object is probably a votive offering or linked in some way to devotional rituals.

Whether an offering or a relic, it has certainly some connection with the building whose ruins compose mound B today.

Dimensions: 43 mm in length; maximux of 12 mm in height; maximum of 16 mm in width.

To our knowledge, no sample of this object has been documented yet.

Observations made on the site, given the preliminary character of the investigation, are necessarily limited. In absence of a stratigraphical context, hypotheses and chronologies are purely provisional, though they are indispensable for a planning of methodological strategies for further research.

Bibliography

Acharya, P.K., *An Encyclopaedia of Hindu Architecture*, Vol. VII, New Delhi, Munshiram Manoharlal, (1946), 1993.

Allchin, B. and Allchin, R.,*The rise of Civilization in India and Pakistan*, New Delhi, Cambridge University Press, 1996.

Allchin, F.R., "City and State Formation in Early Historical South Asia", *South Asian Studies*, 5, 1988/89.

Allchin, F.R. (ed.), *The Archaeology of Early Historic South Asia*, Cambridge, Cambridge Universty Press, 1995.

Bhattacharyya, N.N., *The Geographical Dictionary — Ancient and Early Medieval India*, New Delhi, Munshiram Manoharlal, 1991.

Chandra, M., *Trade and Trade Routes in Ancient India*, New Delhi, Abhinav Publications, 1977.

Dallaporta, A., Filippi, G.G. and Marcolongo, B., "Cercando Kāmpilya", *Asiatica Venetiana*, 1, Univ. "Ca' Foscari"di Venezia, 1996.

Dallaporta, A., Filippi, G.G. and Marcolongo, B., "Kampilya Rediscovered", in *I for Italy*, 5, Embassy of Italy in India, Sept./ Oct. 1996.

Erdösy, G., "Early Historic Cities of Northern India", *South Asian Studies*, 3, 1987.

Ghosh, A., *The City in Early Historical India*, New Delhi, Munshiram Manoharlal, (1973), 1990.

Ghosh, A. (ed.), *An Encyclopaedia of Indian Archaeology*, 2 Vols., New Delhi, Munshiram Manoharlal, 1989.

Gupta, M., *Cultural History of Pāñcāla Janapada from the Earliest Time to 319* BC, A Thesis submitted to Kanpur University for the degree of Doctor of Philosophy, History, 1992.

Indian Archaeology — A Review, 1965-66.

Indian Archaeology — A Review, 1975-76.

Lal Dey, N., *The Geographical Dictionary of Ancient and Medieval India*, New Delhi, Cosmo Publications, (1927), 1979.

Lall, B.B., "Excavations at Hastināpura and other Explorations in Upper Ganga and Sutlej Basins 1950-52", *Ancient India*, 10 & 11.

Narain, A.K. and Roy, T.N., *The Excavations at Prahlādpur (March-April, 1963)*, Vārāṇasī, Banaras Hindu University, 1968.

———, *Excavations at Rājghāṭ (1957-1958; 1960-1965)*, Part I, Vārāṇasī, Banaras Hindu University, 1976.

———, *Excavations at Rājghāṭ (1957-58; 1960-65)*, Part II, Vārāṇasī,

Banaras Hindu University, 1977.

Narain, A.K. and Singh, P., *Excavations at Rājghāṭ (1957-58; 1960-65)*, Part III, Vārānasī, Banaras Hindu University, 1977.

Narain, A.K. and Agrawala, P.K., *Excavations at Rājghāṭ (1957-58; 1960-65)*, Part IV, 2 Vols., Vārāṇasī, Banaras Hindu University, 1978.

Pant, P.C. and Jayaswal, V. (ed.), *Ancient Ceramics — Historical Enquiries & Scientific Approaches*, Delhi, Agam Kala Prakashan, 1997.

Paul, R.K., *South Pāñcāla — A Study in Historical & Cultural Geography*, Kanpur, Sahitya Niketan, 1985.

Possehl, G.L. (ed.), *Harappan Civilisation — A Recent Perspective*, New Delhi, Oxford & IBH, (1982), 1993.

Rangarajan, L.N. (tr.), *The Arthashastra*, New Delhi, Penguin Books, 1992.

Roy, T.N., *The Ganges Civilisation*, New Delhi, Ramanand Vidya Bhavan, 1983.

———, *A Study of Northern Black Polished Ware Culture — An Iron Age Culture of India*, New Delhi, Ramanand Vidya Bhavan, 1986.

Sharma, G.R., *Excavations at Kauśāmbī 1949-50*, Delhi, Memoirs of the Archaeological Survey of India, 74, 1969.

Shrimali, K.M., *History of Pāñcāla*, 2 Vols., New Delhi, Munshiram Manoharlal, 1983.

Shukla, D.N., *Vāstuśāstra — Hindu Science of Architecture*, Vol. I, New Delhi, Munshiram Manoharlal, 1995.

Singh, P., *Excavations at Narhan (1984-89)*, Vārānasī, Banaras Hindu University, 1994.

Sinha, K.K., *Excavations at Sravasti — 1959*, Vārānasī, Banaras Hindu University, 1967.

Singh, S.B., *Archaeology of Pāñcāla Region*, Delhi, Agam Kala Prakashan, 1979.

Tiwari, V.K., "Excavations at Hulāskhera", *Bulletin of Museums & Archaeology U.P.*, pp. 27-8, 1981.

Tripathi, V., *The Painted Grey Ware — An Iron Age Culture of Northern India*, Delhi, Concept Publishing Company, 1976.

———, "A Macro-Level Study of Painted Grey Ware Culture", *Prāgdhārā*, 1, 1990-91.

———, "Iron Age in Uttar Pradesh — Technological Innovation and Social Adaptation", *Prāgdhārā*, 3, 1992-93.

References

1. *Ancient India*, nos. 10-11, 1954-5, pp. 140 and 144.

2. We read: "On the north-western side of the town is a large mound, locally known as Draupadigarh, covering an area of several km square and 5 to 6 m high" (*Indian Archaeology — A Review*, 1965-66, p. 48). Informations about orientation and width of the site are rather inaccurate.
3. *Indian Archaeology — A Review*, 1975-76, pp. 51-2.
4. A similar consistency was observed also in PGW layers of Hastināpura (*Ancient India*, nos. 10-11, 1945-55, p. 14).
5. R.K. Paul, 1958, pp. 69-70.
6. Literally meaning: which provides a ford.
7. See next paragraph.
8. The tract of railway winding along a natural levee south of Kāmpil, may coincide with part of southern branch of the Grand Route.
9. A. Ghosh, (1973) 1990, pp. 54-55.
10. In collaboration with Dr. B. Marcolongo (CNR — Padua).
11. E.g.: Atrañjikhera and Jakhera; some authors date it back to the beginning of the Iron Age.
12. See D.N. Shukla, 1995, p. 288.
13. E.g.: Śiśupālgarh phase III (T.N. Roy 1986, p. 113; A Ghosh, 1989, Vol. 2, p. 413); Ahicchatra phase II (T.N. Roy, 1986, pp. 105-6).
14. E.g.: Ahicchatra phase III and IV (T.N. Roy, 1986, p. 106); Śiśupālgarh phase IV (A. Ghosh, 1989, Vol. 2, p. 413; Kauśāmbī (A. Ghosh, 1989, Vol. 2 pp. 213-14).
15. For simplicity's sake, at least in this preliminary report, we will use the chronologic division adopted by most researchers, though a revision is in progress. The Early Historical Period therefore corresponds to the interval from sixth century BC to fourth century AD; the Late Historical Period (further divided into classic — fourth-seventh century —, post-classic — eighth-ninth century, and early medieval — tenth-eleventh century) corresponds to the period from fourth to twelfth century AD. See A. Ghosh, 1989, Vol. 1, pp. 130-3 and 151-3.
16. F.R. Allchin, (1995, p. 207), shows other fortified towns shaped like a rectangle in some periods of their history, like Mahāsthangarh (Bagura district, Bangladesh), and Kauśāmbī (Allahabad district).
17. See G. Possehl, 1993, Pl. 7. 12.; K.K. Sinha, 1967, fig.13.6.

3

Mahābhārata Reminiscences in Some Villages Near Kāmpil

L. Arnoldo
G. Fuggetta

> "*The village has been the reason for existence of economy, thought, culture, political organisation and settlement in India.*"[1]
>
> **— D.N. Singh**

> "*A village is a way of life, because the people still live more or less as they did before — in spite of contact and communication.*"[2]
>
> **— D.N. Majumdar**

MANY studies on 'Indian village' have been published especially in the period immediately after Independence — a period, as it is obvious, of big changes in the country. However, most of books and articles on this matter have anthropological, social and economic relevance.

We have carried out our research on some villages near Kāmpil in Farrukhābād District (Uttar Pradesh), identified till today with the ancient capital Kāmpilya of the Epic, *Mahābhārata* for their particular location in an area of great archaeological and mythical importance. That is why in this preliminary study we have first developed historical, cultural and religious aspects, hoping to provide in future a more exhaustive image of above-mentioned villages.[3]

We have worked in context of a collaboration between I.R.P.I. (C.N.R. of Padua) and Department of Indological and Far Eastern

Studies of "Ca' Foscari" University of Venice.[4] The area under investigatin is composed of three villages, Māṇikpur, Jhinjauta and Doṇpurā, which belongs to Kāmpil *parganā*,[5] located in Kāimgañj *tahsīl*,[6] the northern most of four *tahsīls*,[7] making up today's Farrukhābād district (about 950 km^2 of extension and 300,000 of peasants). This district originated in 1802 when dominions of *nawābs* of Farrukhābād were joined and given to 'East India Company'; later on it grew up on annexation of other neighbouring territories. To this area of about 100 hc we have to add villages of Pahārpur and Nārāyaṇpur which are most populated sites of Rudāin and Kāmpil. Our study of these last four villages has just started and so our knowledge is limited and not exhaustive.

Historical Outline[8]

The history of the region, that is the present district, goes back to ancient times. The site was inhabited during prehistory, where all bronze age arms, tools and wares have been found all over in this area.[9]

Most ancient inhabitants of the region we know, were the Pāñcāla, allied to the Kuru. The name of people and their country, the Pāñcāla, is not mentioned in the *R̥gveda*. May be their archaic name was Krivi, a R̥gvedic tribe linked to the Kuru. The Krivi, probably, came from lands of Sindhu and Cenāb rivers. Later they moved eastwards crossing the Yamunā as far as Pāñcāla, a land located in Brahmarṣideśa of ancient Āryāvarta, the present districts of Bareilly, Badāūn, Farrukhābād and others. In post-Vedic literature the word Pāñcāla was used both for the land and for its inhabitants.

The traditional history of the district, from ancient times to Bhārata war, comes from the epic, *Mahābhārata* and the Purāṇa. The part of the region we are interested in for our study is situated just south of the river Ganges. It belonged to the reign of South Pāñcāla. Kāmpilya was its capital and Drupad its mythical king. According to Purāṇa, Pāñcāla kings ruling this town were at third place in the list of ten most powerful dynasties from the end of the war of Mahābhārata to Nanda age, but we have no certain information about them. Pāñcāla kingdom was tenth of sixteen most important states in times of Buddha and Mahāvīra when Saṅkiṣa, a town situated on the west edge of the district, became one of the holy places of Buddhism.

Then the region, as well as all of the land of Nanda reign, went under Maurya domination. At that time Pāñcāla started to decline because of numerous civil wars. The historical events that followed up to the time of Gupta emperors are for the most part not known; some coins found in loco which date back to a period from second century BC to third century AD provide some information. So we know that 'Mitra', meaning 'god of the good ruling', was suffixed to names of Pāñcāla kings. It seems that 'Mitra' kings of Pāñcāla were defeated by Kuṣāṇas, during Kaniṣka reign, and they became their vassals.

When in fourth century AD Guptas carried out imperial union of India there was a period of peace and prosperity for the district of Farrukhābād.

The invasion of Hūṇas (512 AD) was the beginning of a disintegration process which brought about foundations of independent kingdoms. In this region, the capital of Kannauj became one of the most important towns in north of India. The Chinese pilgrim Hiuen-Tsang who visited the town in 643, described it as a big and flourishing cosmopolitan centre with hundreds of Buddhist monasteries and more than two hundred Hindu temples. This new capital of Pāñcāla developed more and more under Pratīhāra kingdom, in particular under king Bhoja (836-85).

The first Muslim invasion from Afghanistan at the end of tenth century caused a lot of riots all over the Empire. As a consequence local dynasties became more and more important. We do not exactly know when the independent reign of Kannauj came to an end and when it was annexed to Delhi sultanate. Anyway, the first years of Islamic rule were peaceful enough. But in 1247 local Rājpūts rose against the central power and in 1268 Kāmpil became their stronghold.

Ghiāsuddīn Balban, the then Sultān of Delhi, attacked this town in order to get it freed from rebels. He left his garrisons with Afghan troops in different fortresses built in this area.

We know nothing about the district till 1340 when Muhammad Tughlaq organised an expedition against rebel peasants of Doāb.[10] After a period of peace other wars broke out and Kāmpil was again a centre for Rājpūt resistance; a more serious episode was a rebellion against Mubārak Shāh Saiyid in 1423. Later, the district lived about twenty-five years peacefully but it was weakened by a terrible famine. Then Lodī and Mughal dynasties ruled the country. When Auraṅgzeb died (1707), the Muslim power in northern India began to decline and a lot of independent principalities were established. Among them Farrukhābād district is an important part in history with respect to both periods, before and after Independence of the country from British rule.

We did not find written documents about origin of villages under investigation in order to go back to the process of establishment and evolution of settlements. That is why we got data from oral tradition, stories handed down from father to son in which some events of past, which are common in the history of the whole district, get mixed, sometimes with diachronic incongruities, with some episodes of ancient mythology. Anyway, all of the present inhabitants of these villages keep in their mind those *Mahābhārata* reminiscences which are just suitable to geographical morphology of the area. On the contrary, other settlements close to them do not know about *Mahābhārata* themes, which we have considered in our research. This fact greatly points out features peculiar to that oral tradition. Of course, we took care to distinguish between the true oral tradition of a community and a tradition influenced by local secularised institutions. For example, at Kāmpil there are a great number of graduated people (B.A. or M.A.); there is a Middle School and a Secondary High School near Kāimgañj; in consequence of all those we think that some of the information about *Mahābhārata* places come from a revision of the oral tradition by the erudite class.

We carefully checked all of the information obtained from Kāmpil. Most of them were spurious and not usable. On the contrary in villages of Māṇikpur, Jhinjauta and Doṇpurā the oral tradition was highly reliable and certainly the result of a regular transmission. A small number of teachers teach how to read and write in elementary schools of Māṇikpur and Jhinjauta.[11] They do not have any deep historical-religious training. When we asked them about mythical geography of the place, they gave same answers as that of their illiterate fellow countrymen. We think it is same for villages of Pahārpur and Nārāyaṇpur as there are no schools. While we cannot give any opinion on Rudāin. Apart from that we have to consider another important aspect of the oral tradition, typically Indian. We mean oral tradition at learned level which can control, correct and adapt the ordinary oral tradition. For our area investigation, this learned tradition is assured by *paṇḍit* Candrabhānu Śāstrī living in the village of Jhinjauta. He is ninety-five years old but his mind is lively and sharp. This old brāhmaṇa has great oral knowledge of the Śruti and the Smṛti and he maintains a depth of judgement characteristic of Advaita *karpatrian* environment. His version of oral data cannot be compared to that of his fellow countrymen, who are more or less illiterate. It is a re-reading of the oral popular tradition according to the highest learned tradition in which he adds to the knowledge of *Mahābhārata* the cognition of different Śāstras and Purāṇas. *Paṇḍit* Śāstrījī does not know English; he achieved his studies in Sanskrit in Benares under the guidance of *paṇḍits*, *ācāryas* and *gurus*, according to the oral sacredotal tradition. His reliable contribution has been separately considered from other oral traditions. In the area under investigation the *paṇḍit* and members of his family are only people who represent the cognitive tradition (*jñāna-kāṇḍa*) as the other brāhmaṇas of the area are simply *pujāris* devoted to the ritual (*karma-kāṇḍa*).

Geographical Landscape and Morphology of the Village

As soon as we move northwards from the town of Kāimgañj to meet the ancient branch of the Gaṅgā, the Būḍhīgaṅgā, the rural landscape becomes pre-eminent. This territory, like the rest of the district, is flat with light undulations and slopes.[12] A kind of upland, cut by the erosive action of rivers, slopes with a steep scarp on the Gaṅgā plain that follows the boundary of Kāimgañj tahsīl in its northern and oriental part. Connected to the dynamic river system of Gaṅgā[13] a series of channels have the task of draining surplus water at the end of the monsoon season.[14]

Gardens with melons and water-melons, groves with tamarind, papaya and mango trees, for which *tahsīl* is well known, alternate for plantations. The vast natural forests of Middle Ages or big rows of tall plants which bordered big roads of the Mughal Empire are not to be found any more.[15]

Only after 1857, the British started a programme of partial

forest plantation for which most of old trees of the district were dated from 1870. In consequence of disappearance of big wooded areas there was a substantial diminution of the wild fauna towards complete extinction[16], while the bird fauna is rich and big reptiles are common. It is not rare to see very nice little families of cranes or herons in the background of paddy fields or small ponds, and of course we must have been lucky to catch a glimpse of one of the last crocodiles of the river Gaṅgā.

Leaving then the *parganā* of Kāmpil and proceeding westwards we cross more and more narrow roads; the asphalt a little at a time disappears and we must travel on disconnected earthen footsteps, till we are obliged to leave our car and proceed on foot. We walk along small banks which bind fields well cultivated with tobacco, cereals or potatoes;[17] we cross yellow fields of ripe mustard taking care not to trample seedlings and with a fear of meeting snakes (in this period of the year, February, they are still in hibernation). The sight, closed by vast expanses of sugarcane, suddenly opens on small villages which at the beginning seem all alike grey and dusty as they are because of clay, but after repeated viewings, we could easily recognise and distinguish one from the other.

In any case the welcome, at first timid and a little bit uncertain, becomes warmer but never intrusive. The hospitality is very kind and it is difficult to refuse such nice invitations for a cup of tea under a shady porch, sitting on a typical *cārpāī* and surrounded by a coloured crowd of adults and children. We listen to stories of events that carry us back to a remote past, sometimes distorted or enriched by imagination, but deeply rooted in their memory. The memory of ancient origins, which according to them go back to *Mahābhārata* times, seems to confer upon them a dignity in some way dimmed by daily hard work.[18] Also everyone is disposed to give information on the actual structure and religious and social organisation of villages. While we are crossing the narrow lanes with an escort of happy children of all ages, what initially appears like an incoherent agglomeration of huts and small houses of mud, acquires a functional order and it is possible to identify quarters, handicraft shops and religious areas.

The sub-division of the community in a more or less big number of castes is reflected in the organisation of rural settlement,[19] as we can notice in Jhinjauta and Māṇikpur. In the village of Doṇpurā the presence of an only śūdra caste justifies the uniformity of its poor houses and rural structures. In all of the villages we visited most of diffused dwellings have walls of mixed mud and clay and roof of straw. It is made up of an only room that sometimes has a porch opening into a small courtyard. Despite their poverty these houses are generally clean and tidy. In big villages there are also houses having more rooms distributed around a central square court, typical of big families. The house shows economic condition of its inhabitants and people more well-to-do have brick houses with fenced courtyard that opens on the road through wooden front doors with carved decorations. Walls are often decorated with painted figures of animals, mythical characters and divinities. On front walls or on portals a series of imprints of hands in black could be seen. They are painted on new buildings so that buildings appear old and ugly in order to keep away wicked envious spirits. If hands are imprinted in red they are of good omen.

Some scenes which stand out in relief on walls of some villages, as we can see in Māṇikpur, are very interesting. They have two principal characters, one masculine and one feminine, and other small ones, in front of which the marriage of two puppets is mimed. After this representation the true marriage between two young people of the village is arranged. Generally, there are several of such reliefs in every village, each on a house wall of the present caste.

Getting out from the maze of lanes you could find yourself in open areas among houses (not real little squares), in the centre of which there is the traditional sacred tree, generally the *pīpal* (Ficus religiosa) or the *bargad* (Ficus bengalensis).[20] It is the tree abode of the tutelary divinities of the village, around which inhabitants put the sacred stone images which are object of their veneration. These small sculptures and reliefs, found by chance during work in the field, are placed inside temples or around sacred trees or in houses for daily *pūjā*. Some of them are of huge archaeological interest and therefore useful for reconstruction of the history of the territory.

Mahābhārata Reminiscences

The big village of Kāmpil (about 6000 inhabitants) rises above a conspicuous mound, eight meters over the alluvial plain. This oval mound (700 m × 300 m long) is situated along a scarp that descends suddenly to plain. At the eastern side of the mound, under the steep slope lies the ancient course of the river Ganges, an abandoned meander now reduced to a small swamp of one hundred forty meters, along which there are *ghāṭ*s of sixteenth century. The river, that now flows four kilometres farther to north-east, would have moved later. Besides it remains a rectangular pool with steps for ablutions, called Draupadī Kuṇḍ. The north-eastern end of the mound is surmounted by two buildings. The first is a little temple to which inhabitants consider *samādhi* of *ṛṣi* Kapila, who would have given name to the city. Instead, clearly, it is a little temple that contains a *śivaliṅga*, dedicated to the *yakṣa* Kapila. The second building, unfortunately recently restored, contains in the *garbhagṛha* a very old *śivaliṅga*, which inhabitants, and the *pujārī* particularly, relate to *Rāmāyaṇa*. This temple stands on a *dharamśālā* and an annex where the *pujārī* lives. They assert that Draupadī Kuṇḍ is the pond from which Draupadī would have emerged as young girl, seated on a lotus with a miraculous *liṅgam* in her hand. This is an episode of *Mahābhārata* located in Kāmpil to which other villages also recognise. On the other hand, identification of walls rising at south-west extremity of mound with walls of the city of Kāmpilya, capital of South Pāñcāla, cannot be supported in any way, as they are remains of a Mughal fortification, probably of sixteenth century. The mound is large and reserves many surprises for future. The other 'oral' tradition in Kāmpil concerns with the birth and illumination of thirteenth Jain *tīrthaṅkara* and therefore they are set out of the epic tradition.

More suitable and useful results can be obtained from the study of oral traditions of Māṇikpur, Jhinjauta and Doṇpurā, rural villages which are separated from each other by a vast field of archaeological remains.

Māṇikpur is a village of about thousand people. The head of this community is Sureś Candra Pāṇḍey, a forty-year old, and Devasinghjī, a ninety-year-old, is considered the wisest person. These people were most reliable authorities for information. In this village four principal castes live in separate areas. The śūdras, the most numerous group, are situated north-west; the brāhmaṇas live in south-western part; the kṣatriya, less numerous, are settled south-east; the only family of vaiśyas is in north-east of the village.

At the border of the village there are four or five Bañjārā families, nowadays converted to Islam and two Kalābāj families apparently Hindu. They live in huts out of the village, but they are not considered as untouchables. It seems that in this area no remarkable social and ethnic tensions have taken place. This could be a sign of an ancient peaceful cohabitation between Hindus and tribals, peculiar in Kāmpilya of *Mahābhārata* age. Bañjārās live on breeding of buffaloes and pigs while Kalābāj now a days are traders in small household articles or are musicians and dancers in fairs. Men dress-up as women for dancing performances. An elderly *vairāginī* also belongs to Kalābāj community. She is a follower of Gorakh Nāth and is regularly dressed in orange, with a *rudrākṣa-mālā* around her neck.

The prevailing activity among inhabitants of the village is agriculture. Also kṣatriya, to whom the title of *ṭhākur* is conferred, participate in humblest agricultural menial jobs. In Māṇikpur potter's activity[21] is very important, as we can see from the presence, in a relatively small community, of two families engaged in such works.[22]

In front of their houses, in the main little square, vases, bowls of clay and toys for children are put to desiccate. When we arrived there on a holiday one of them was proud to give us a demonstration of his ability in moulding some object at the wheel. He used a type of wheel which is widespread in Uttar Pradesh, so-called 'socketed block-wheel', that is a wheel, in this case in stone,[23] with a hollow in its low part, in which a pivot is inserted. This pivot is made of tamarind wood and shaped in a rough cone buried in earth from which it emerges around 5-10 cm.

The manufacture of pottery is even now, in this area of Uttar Pradesh, a hereditary occupation, the monopoly of a group or caste, śūdra[24], tightly connected to the society and economy of the village. The joint family is the main productive unit. In recent times 'Industries Department of the Government' has looked for, but without success, organising cooperative societies of potters in order to increase production and to control prices. All members of the family or of the subcaste involved in this activity, cooperate, according to sex and age, above all in getting the raw material and in firing vessels. Men perform heaviest jobs while women act as assistants and in some places, but not in U.P., they decorate the pottery. Children learn from their parents and when they use wheel for the first time, even if there is no real ceremony of initiation, incense and sweets will be offered to the wheel. There is a universal taboo: women cannot work at the wheel.

In Uttar Pradesh potters generally go from village to village selling their manufactured articles. When the *yajmānī*[25] system was in use the potter had his customers with whom he exchanged his pottery for services and other products. Now the system of barter is no more or is about to go.

In different regions of north different terms used for potter are *kumbhāra*, *kumhāra*, *kubhāra*, *kumār* and *kumor*. Etymologically all these words are derived from the Sanskrit *kumbha* (*ku*, earth) that means vase; for this reason *kumbhakāraḥ* is 'the potter'.

Hindu *kumhāras* call themselves *prajāpat* or *prajāpati* from the Vedic Prajāpati, Lord of Creatures.[26]

The legend is as follows

> Once Brahmā shared sugarcane among his sons and each of them ate his part, but Kumhāra, who was completely absorbed in his work, forgot to eat. The piece that he had preserved near his block of clay put out roots and soon a plant of sugarcane grew. Some days later, when Brahmā asked his sons for some sugarcane, nobody could give it to him, except Kumhāra who offered him the whole plant. Brahmā was happy because of devotion of the potter to his work and gave him the title of 'Prajāpati'.

In the whole of north India potters worship their utensils during particular festivities and the orthodox ones also do their *pūjā* every morning before going to work. The wheel-worship by the potter in this part of India seems to be a relic of the symbolic worship of the Sun, whose most ancient name is Prajāpati. Potters' caste, like that of artisans, is facing a crisis without precedents in attempt of preserving its traditional techniques and fighting innovations.

A new type of rural economy, that emerged after Independence in 1947, has caused a crisis in the system of traditional division of jobs in Hindu society. The occupational mobility of caste, also not being a modern phenomenon, is being developed more and more. Nowadays a member of the potter caste could get a different job but maintains the sense of affiliation with his caste and will always declare himself a member of it. This is the case, in the village of Māṇikpur, of Rūplāl Kumār who does not practice the work of his caste, being a well-to-do landowner. He is seen as a descendant of the Kaddhi Kumār who gave hospitality to the five Pāṇḍavas when they participated, disguised as brāhmaṇas, in the tournament *svayaṁvara* in honour of Draupadī. This is also corroborated by Gaṅgādīn, the *pujārī* of Durgā *mandir*, the most important temple of the village. The presence of descendants of Kaddhi Kumār in Māṇikpur allows inhabitants to hand down legends concerning the *svayaṁvara* of Draupadī. They affirm that the competition was held on the shore of a little pond with clear water, the Vedutāla, situated half km north of Doṇpurā. It is a vein of water, surrounded by a grove, connected to the course of the Ganges, that flows about six km north-east from this place. Near Vedutāla a *melā* and a *darśana* were performed until 1992-93. Then the place was abandoned because of episodes of brigandage in its environs.

Doṇpurā is a minuscule village with about a hundred inhabitants. The head of the village considers inhabitants as pertaining to śūdra caste. The kṣatriyas of Jhinjauta consider them as vaiśyas because they sell products of their job. They define themselves as kṣatriyas and have added to their name Śākya with the suffix Singh, meaning lion.[27] They seem to have a tribal origin, which would explain the confusion among inhabitants of surrounding villages regarding their caste definition. The village is poorest in the area and maintains itself on agriculture. Women of the village weave baskets with motley straw but they do not commercialise their products.

According to the local tradition Doṇpurā would derive its name from *ṛṣi* Dhaumya, who was the *guru* of Pāṇḍavas and had his *āśrama* in that place. Also in Doṇpurā the legend regarding *svayaṁvara* is important. But in this village the bad fame of Vedutāla is not attributed to brigands but to the presence of a *pīpal* tree, the abode of a *brahmabābā*, also called *brahmadevatā* or *brahmarākṣasa*. It is the soul in torment, the *piśāca* of a brāhmaṇa who, condemned to a terrestrial exile because of his sins during life, remains in this world operating in wicked forms. Those people, above all children, who perform actions against *dharma* in the vicinity of *pīpal*, are possessed by the demon. In the village of Doṇpurā a certain Rāmpāl also lives who, in trance, has the power of exorcising children, forcing the *brahmarākṣasa* to return to the *pīpal* tree. He, possessed by the goddess Kālī or by the god Poṭṭu,[28] oracles. Rāmpāl evidently suffers from psychic disorders: he appears absent, hallucinated, withered brusquely from a pacific state to anger. He is homosexual and lame, but these conditions do not upset all his fellow townspersons. He falls into a trance whenever he wishes, in the daytime, preferably on Friday or on Saturday. Standing in an erect position he begins to quiver, and is forced to jump on the place. Sometimes he uses incense sticks sniffing their perfume. When possessed by the goddess or by the god he becomes calm, sits down, and answers questions with a clear and authoritative voice. Either in his ordinary state or in his lucid trance, Rāmpāl transmits an anxious personality. Kālī and Poṭṭu, that is to say Mahiṣāsura, divinities who possess this oracle, are particularly important for *Mahābhārata* myth. A hypostasis of Śiva is the celestial husband of the goddess Kālī, who descends on earth in form of Draupadī and Mahiṣāsura.

Jhinjauta is the biggest of three villages. The caste majority is represented by kṣatriyas. The brāhmaṇas live in the centre of the village surrounded by kṣatriyas of Pr̥thvi Cauhān origin. There are also some families of Rājpūts originally from Jaipur. There are no vaiśyas. Our most important informants have been *paṇḍit* Śāstrījī, *Ṭhākurs* — Choṭesingh, Lallusingh, Bhīmasingh and Gugubhakasingh. Majority of inhabitants live on agriculture, but many of them have served in Army as officers or in the government administration. Also in Jhinjauta an identical story regarding the *svayaṁvara* at Vedutāla is told. Only Śāstrījī adds that the blood of the fish reached by the arrow of Arjuna squirted up to Rudāin which in ancient times was known by the name of Rudraprayāg, the red confluence. Śāstrījī also affirms that Rudraprayāg was an ancient place sacred to eleven Rudras, which, in the *Śatapatha Brāhmaṇa*, have been interpreted as eleven vital breaths.[29] This statement puts that place in relationship with death and funeral rites. In fact, according to the *Mahābhārata* tradition, Pāṇḍavas would have reached Rudraprayāg to perform *tapas* and offer *piṇḍa-dāna* in honour of their father Pāṇḍu. The offer must be performed during *amāvasyā*, the night of new moon when it falls on Monday. This coincidence was accustomed to happen once a year in *dvāpara yuga*. But on that occasion the celestial conjunction did not present itself for twelve years, therefore Pāṇḍavas cursed a personified *amāvasyā* and condemned him to rarer apparitions in the course in *kali yuga*. The *tapas* performed by Pāṇḍavas had the sacred pond called Sardhipaktāl for scenery. Till today Rudāin is the destination of a pilgrimage and a *mela* is organised when it happens to be *amāvasyā*. Whoever takes bath on that night purifies himself from every sin. The place is particularly consecrated to funeral rites and the tradition reiterates that the *piṇḍa-dāna* performed on the shores of the pond has more effectiveness than the one performed at Gayā.

Between Māṇikpur and Jhinjauta there is a little pond of irregular form, called Dharmatāl, Dharmaśāla or Dharmahuta, which is surrounded by a row of bricks that presupposes a rich antiquity of the site. In the lake an islet of modest proportion appears. In this place one finds ashes and burnt seeds of ancient sacrifices and the population of Jhinjauta assert that this was the place where King Drupad performed *yajña*. They affirm that the name of Jhinjauta is corrupt form of the Sanskrit term *yajñahotra*. To this lake is also connected the figure of Yudhiṣṭhira as Dharmarāja. This brings us back to the motive of the cult of corpses because Dharmarāja is another name of god Yama.[30] The references to this lake are particularly scheming and mysterious, as the proximity of the abode of Dhaumya to the lake allows an identification of Dharmatāl with the mythical Dharmakūpa pond on whose shores a talk between Yudhiṣṭhira and Dhaumya would have been set.

About four hundred meters from the lake east-south-east direction, there is a small mound, very similar to the ancient pre-Buddhist *stūpas*. This is particularly a revered place, because it is considered to be the *samādhi* of one of the five survivors of the Bhārata war. The warrior really, would stay drowsy inside the mound, waiting for the end of the *kali yuga*. Owing to this privilege of an extraordinary longevity, the inhabitants of villages have conferred upon him the title of *ṛṣi*. A certain Kṛpāsingh, father of Navābsingh and grandfather of living

Kṛṣṇasingh, inhabitant of Jhinjauta, discovered the mound about sixty years ago and he testified it to have found inside the *ṛṣi* covered by a manger similar to a big bowl, in the form of those still used in the area. The mysterious person if awaken from his *tapas* would want a drink. Amazed by the blue colour of water, the *ṛṣi* refused it because it did not have the milky appearance of the Ganges water, as during *dvāpara yuga*. Having made a dictum, he covered himself again and continued his uninterrupted *tapas*, waiting for the imminent end of the dark age. This episode is commented upon by villagers, and because of the prodigy, the tumulus is the object of a cult and of *pradakṣiṇā* rites. Another contemporary legend tells that until 1964 it was not infrequent, in the night, to meet the five survivors of the Mahābhārata war after crossing the path from Sardhipaktāl to this place. It has been impossible to understand why inhabitants of Jhinjauta mention these dates with so much of assurance. A more recent extraordinary episode that happened in 1987 was told by Surendra who is now thirty years old. He had approached the Vedutāl pond at dawn, because of a rite of purification to be performed in those waters before dawn. It allows one to express a wish with a guarantee of its being granted. Arriving there he met five *ṛṣis* while they were performing ablutions. One of them noticed his inopportune presence, provoking his escape. However we may judge these episodes, also it appears useful to underline these local traditions based on the Epic.

Changes in the post-Independence Period

Despite the presence of archaism in the life of villages it appears evident that important changes have already taken place or are taking place at all levels of the rural society in the years following Independence.

The urban influence has increased, depending on the distance of the village from the city or from bigger centres or in relationship to the development of the road network. Actually the village as a completely independent unit is a myth; in fact it has always been a part of a wider entity. In any case villages in India, before the British Rāj, were less dependent economically from cities than today's. "Zamindari Abolition and Land Reforms Act", applied in our District in July 1952, has produced meaningful changes in social and economic life of the people. The elite of *zamīndārs*[31] has been supplanted by the community of growers who possess their own land and work on them. Farmers of visited villages affirm their possession of land for cultivation even if for some it is hardly sufficient to survive. Little by little new technologies (irrigation systems, fertilizers), etc. are introduced. Only in one village we find a person possessing a tractor and that is proudly shown.

Even if the classical system of relationships between castes or the *jajmānī* in rural areas is changing, as we could verify in the investigated villages, the bond to the caste traditions of the past is still strong.[32] Also the *pañcāyat*, that is the council of elders of each caste, reunite to level any controversy if among its members, is losing power. However, still today, the habit to consult more educated and wise people to resolve critical situations persists in our villages as well.

In the field of education a big effort is being made against illiteracy. In all villages, except the smallest one, Doṇpurā, there is at least a primary school. But more arduous battle is fought every year against excess of water that floods wide zones during monsoon season or on the contrary against the drought that strikes the District in particular years. During monsoons the so-called catchment areas are affected by erosion. Because of this, lands close to banks of water courses, particularly the Ganges, become unusable and thus cultivable areas of villages change. Besides, big zones of the District are flooded for long periods after the end of the monsoon, becoming lakes or accumulations of drains of superficial water. The more external parts of these depressions, when not flooded, are planted with rice and bowline. The inundation provokes a serious degradation of the soil which is covered with salty efflorescences, above all carbonate of sodium. To face and resolve all these problems in this District a programme for soil preservation is being carried out since years 1964-65.[33] A diffused system of channels for irrigation, which drain water from rivers, wells, hydraulic ducts punctuate the rural landscape so that the periods of drought can not be faced with safety. The opening of channels of irrigation, beginning from the last century, has produced a marked improvement in techniques and models of cultivation, allowing an evident increase in harvests which, as usual in Doāb, comprises of *rabī* (spring crop of wheat, bowline, chickpeas, mustard, etc.), *kharīf* (autumn crop of cereals, corn, rice, vegetables, etc.) and *zaid* (additional cultures). The practice, very wide spread in the past, of leaving fields uncultivated for at least a season has been abandoned and replaced with crop rotation. Also the industry is receiving a certain impulse, even if tightly tied to agriculture.

References

1. In F. Farinelli (ed.), *Il villaggio indiano*, Milano 1981.
2. D.N. Majumdar, *Caste and Communication in an Indian Village*, Bombay, 1958.
3. According to R.P.B. Singh, (1974), 'village' means not only the inhabited area but also the cultivated fields depending on it.
4. The study has been co-financed and coordinated by V.A.I.S. in collaboration with D.A.V. College of the University of Kanpur and the Pāñcāla Research Institute of Kanpur.
5. Sub-district in an administrative division.
6. Sub-division of a district for fiscal purposes.
7. The other three districts are Farrukhābād, Chibrāmau and Kannauj.
8. P. Mishra (ed.), *Uttar Pradesh District Gazetteers*, Lucknow, 1988.
9. In the Kāmpil region was found PGW (grey and painted grey ware), similar to those found in Hastināpura, and NBP (northern black polished ware).
10. It is the land between the Gaṅgā and Yamunā confluence.
11. At Doṇpurā there is not to be found any kind of school.
12. The mid height of these reliefs is around 150 m on the Gangetic plain.
13. The river continuously changes its course, slowly and gradually, and it can maintain the same direction for many years. At the beginning of this century it constituted the northern boundary of the district while now it flows northwards of Kāimgañj *tahsīl*, with a tendency to return to its old bed.
14. Monsoon seasons last from about middle of June to the end of September.
15. The 'royal road of the Maurya', that became the 'Bādśāhī road' in Muslim period, connected the ancient capitals of Kannauj and Prayāg and it was the main artery that crossed north India from the far east to the north-western frontier, beyond Taxilā. The ancient city of Kāmpilya was on this road which can be considered the precursor of today's 'Grand Trunk Road'.

16. The last tiger was seen in 1803.
17. The district of Farrukhābād tops in production of potatoes in the state of U.P.
18. Prof. A. Misra of D.A.V. College of the University of Kanpur kindly acted as our interpreter.
19. M.K. Marriott: *Village India: Studies in the Little Community*, Chicago, 1958.
20. Another sacred tree, the *tulsī* (Ocimum sanctum), is instead more often near single houses, possibly on elevated position.
21. B. Saraswati, *Pottery-Making Cultures and Indian Civilization*, New Delhi, 1979.
22. There is only one other potter in the town of Kāmpil.
23. In the past it was also of raw clay.
24. *Manu Saṁhitā*.
25. *Jajmānī* or *yajmānī* was the classical system of relationships between different castes in a village: classes not labouring in fields were used to provide special services to farmers in exchange for food and other natural products. Now this system of personal exchanges has been replaced by contractual impersonal relationships.
26. Also in the old village of Kishan Garh, district of Aligarh, the potter is called *prajāpat*.
27. Śākya is the Sanskrit term for Shitian tribes.
28. In the whole of the District there are three principal classes of grounds: *dūmaṭ* or loam, *maṭiyār* or clay, *bhūr* or sand.
29. "Who are Rudras? They are ten vital spirits in man, and *ātman* is eleventh. When they all together leave the deadly body they provoke a moan, *rud*. That is why they are called Rudras." — *ŚB*, XI.6.3.7. It is also evident that *paṇḍit* Śāstrījī uses indifferently the etymology of Rudra meaning to moan, to howl, according to *Nirukta* tradition, and the etymology evoking red colour.
30. *Skanda Purāṇa*, III.2.4.88.
31. In origin, fiscal collectors in the Mughal system, with the advent of the English rule, became landowners and the farmers their tenants.
32. Some restrictions of the caste system remain: For instance, the case of marriage which cannot be allowed in outer
33. In the whole District there are three principal classes of terrain: *dūmaṭ* or loam, *maṭiyār* or clay, *bhūr* or sand.

The Contributors

L. Arnoldo: Indologist, Researcher of V.A.I.S.

Annamaria Dallaporta: Archaeologist, Researcher and Secretary General of V.A.I.S.

G. Fuggetta: Indologist, Researcher of V.A.I.S.

Lucio Marcato: Archaeologist, Professor of Archaeology of India, University "Ca' Foscari" of Venice.

Bruno Marcolongo: Geo-archaeologist, Director of Research Unit/National Research Council of Padua and Academician of V.A.I.S.